HOW CEO'S DECIDE

UNVEILING THE DECISION-MAKING PROCESS OF BUSINESS LEADERS

AMIT GUPTA

Made with ♥ on the Notion Press Platform
www.notionpress.com

Contents

Dedication

To my esteemed mentor, Mr. Sunil Goyal,

This book is dedicated to you, the guiding light who has illuminated my path in the world of entrepreneurship. Your wisdom, unwavering support, and insightful guidance have been instrumental in shaping my journey from a fledgling entrepreneur to a seasoned business leader. Your teachings have not only influenced my decisions but have also inspired the ethos with which I approach both business and life.

Your belief in my potential and your relentless encouragement have been my anchor, especially during times of doubt and challenge. This book, "How CEOs Decide," is a testament to the principles and values you have imparted to me. It encapsulates the essence of decision-making that you have so profoundly exemplified.

Thank you for being my guru, mentor, and father-like figure. Your impact on my life is immeasurable, and for that, I am eternally grateful.

With deepest respect and gratitude,

Amit Gupta

Foreword

In the dynamic and ever-evolving world of business, the role of a CEO extends far beyond traditional leadership. It is a position that demands a unique blend of vision, resilience, and strategic acumen. As a serial entrepreneur, I have had the privilege of experiencing the complexities and nuances of this role firsthand. This book, "How CEOs Decide," is an exploration of the critical decision-making processes that define successful leadership.

The genesis of this book lies in my personal journey—one that began with a bold decision to leave the security of a conventional job and embark on the exhilarating path of entrepreneurship. My experiences have taught me that the decisions made in the boardroom echo far beyond the confines of the office, impacting employees, stakeholders, and the broader community. The weight of these decisions necessitates a profound understanding of both the art and science of decision-making.

Throughout my career, I have been fortunate to cross paths with some of the most influential and inspiring leaders. Their stories, insights, and strategies have significantly contributed to the perspectives shared within these pages. Each chapter delves into the minds of these exceptional individuals, unveiling the frameworks and thought processes that guide their decisions.

This book is not just a manual for aspiring CEOs; it is a narrative that weaves together real-world experiences, practical advice, and theoretical insights. Whether you are a seasoned executive, an emerging leader, or simply someone with an interest in the intricacies of business leadership, this book aims to provide valuable takeaways that can be applied across various contexts.

I would like to extend my heartfelt gratitude to my mentor, Mr. Sunil Goyal, whose unwavering support and guidance have been a cornerstone of my entrepreneurial journey. His influence is deeply embedded in the principles discussed in this book.

As you embark on this reading journey, I encourage you to reflect on the decisions you make in your own life and career. Consider how you can apply the lessons learned from the distinguished leaders featured in this book to enhance your decision-making abilities and drive meaningful impact in your own spheres of influence.

Thank you for joining me in exploring the fascinating world of how CEOs decide.ee

With warm regards,

Amit Gupta

Preface

The journey of writing this book, "How CEOs Decide," has been as enlightening and transformative as the entrepreneurial path that inspired it. From the early days of my career, I have been fascinated by the pivotal moments that define successful leadership. The decisions made by CEOs not only shape the trajectory of their organizations but also influence industries and economies on a broader scale.

As a serial entrepreneur, I have encountered a diverse array of challenges and opportunities. Each experience has reinforced the importance of sound decision-making, a skill that is both an art and a science. The inspiration for this book emerged from my desire to understand and demystify the decision-making processes of the world's most successful CEOs. What drives their choices? How do they navigate uncertainty and complexity? What frameworks do they rely on to steer their companies toward success?

To answer these questions, I embarked on a journey of exploration and discovery, engaging with a wide spectrum of business leaders, mentors, and industry experts. Their insights and experiences form the backbone of this book, offering readers a comprehensive look into the minds of top executives.

Throughout the chapters, you will find a blend of personal anecdotes, case studies, and practical strategies. This holistic approach is designed to provide a well-rounded perspective on decision-making, one that is both accessible and deeply informative. Whether you are an aspiring entrepreneur, a seasoned executive, or someone with a keen interest in business leadership, this book aims to equip you with the tools and knowledge to make more informed and impactful decisions.

I owe a debt of gratitude to Mr. Sunil Goyal, my mentor and guide, whose wisdom and support have been invaluable throughout my journey. His teachings have profoundly influenced my approach to business and leadership, and his impact is woven throughout the pages of this book.

Writing "How CEOs Decide" has been a labor of love, driven by a passion to share the lessons I have learned and the insights I have gathered. It is my hope that this book will serve as a valuable resource, inspiring and guiding readers as they navigate their own leadership journeys.

Thank you for embarking on this journey with me. May you find the wisdom and inspiration within these pages to make decisions that lead to success and fulfillment.

With sincere appreciation,

Amit Gupta

Acknowledgements

Writing "How CEOs Decide" has been a deeply rewarding experience, and it would not have been possible without the support and contributions of many remarkable individuals. I am immensely grateful to everyone who has played a part in bringing this book to life.

First and foremost, I extend my heartfelt gratitude to my mentor, Mr. Sunil Goyal. Your unwavering support, guidance, and wisdom have been the cornerstone of my entrepreneurial journey. Your influence is deeply woven into the fabric of this book, and I am forever thankful for your mentorship.

A special thanks to my family and friends, whose love and encouragement have been my anchor throughout this journey. To my parents, for instilling in me the values of hard work and perseverance. To my spouse, for your unwavering support, understanding, and patience during the many late nights and long weekends spent working on this book. And to my children, for being a constant source of joy and inspiration.

I am also grateful to my team, whose dedication and hard work have been instrumental in the creation of this book. Your expertise and attention to detail have ensured that every aspect of this project was executed flawlessly. A special thank you to my editor, whose insightful feedback and meticulous editing have greatly enhanced the quality of this book.

To my colleagues and peers in the entrepreneurial community, thank you for your camaraderie and the shared experiences that have enriched my understanding of leadership and decision-making. Your support and collaboration have been invaluable.

Credits: I extend my sincere appreciation to Ms. Avee Goyal, whose thorough research has provided a strong foundation for this book, and to Ms. Anee Goyal, whose meticulous proofreading has ensured clarity and precision in the manuscript. Your contributions have been vital to the completion of this project.

Finally, I would like to thank my readers. Your interest and enthusiasm for understanding the intricacies of leadership and decision-making have been the driving force behind this book. It is my sincere hope that "How CEOs Decide" will inspire and empower you to make informed and impactful decisions in your own leadership journeys.

With deep appreciation,

Amit Gupta

Prologue

In the world of business, decisions are the keystones that build the edifice of success. Every choice, from the seemingly trivial to the profoundly strategic, has the potential to shape the future of a company. As I reflect on my own entrepreneurial journey, I am reminded of the myriad decisions that have defined my path—some triumphant, others humbling, but all instructive.

The idea for "How CEOs Decide" germinated from a deep-seated curiosity about the decision-making processes of top leaders. What distinguishes a successful CEO from the rest? How do they navigate the intricate web of challenges and opportunities that come their way? These questions fueled my quest to uncover the underlying principles and practices that drive effective leadership.

My journey began early, with a bold step away from a conventional job and into the uncertain yet exhilarating realm of entrepreneurship. Along the way, I encountered mentors, peers, and industry stalwarts whose wisdom and experience provided invaluable guidance. Among them, Mr. Sunil Goyal stands out as a beacon of inspiration. His mentorship has profoundly influenced my approach to decision-making, instilling in me the confidence and clarity to face complex business challenges.

In this prologue, I invite you to join me on an exploration of the decision-making landscape. This book is not merely a collection of theories and methodologies; it is a narrative woven from real-life experiences and insights from some of the most accomplished CEOs in the business world. Through candid interviews, case studies, and personal reflections, I aim to present a holistic view of how leaders make choices that steer their organizations toward success.

Each chapter delves into a specific aspect of decision-making, offering a blend of strategic frameworks and practical advice. You will find stories of resilience, innovation, and calculated risk-taking—each illustrating the multifaceted nature of leadership. By examining these stories, my hope is that you will gain a deeper understanding of the cognitive processes and emotional intelligence that underpin effective decision-making.

This prologue sets the stage for a journey of discovery. It is a journey that transcends industries and geographies, capturing the essence of what it means to lead with purpose and conviction. Whether you are at the helm of a multinational corporation, leading a startup, or aspiring to climb the corporate ladder, the lessons contained within these pages are designed to inspire and empower you.

As you turn the pages of "How CEOs Decide," I encourage you to reflect on your own decision-making experiences. Consider how the insights shared by these exemplary leaders can be applied to your unique context. Leadership is not a destination but a continuous journey of learning and growth, and it is my sincere hope that this book will serve as a trusted companion on your path to success.

Welcome to an exploration of the art and science of decision-making.

Amit Gupta

Message From Author

Dear Aspiring Entrepreneur,

Thank you for picking up "How CEOs Decide: The Art of Taking Decisions." This book is a product of my own experience and deep dive into the minds of some of the most successful and influential CEOs of our time. As a young entrepreneur, you are at the threshold of a journey filled with challenges, opportunities, and countless decisions that will shape the future of your venture.

In writing this book, my goal was to provide you with a roadmap—a guide to understanding the complex decision-making processes that drive the success of top executives. Through interviews, case studies, and thorough analysis, I have sought to uncover the principles, strategies, and mental frameworks that distinguish great leaders.

The path of entrepreneurship is rarely straightforward. It demands resilience, creativity, and the ability to make informed decisions under uncertainty. This book aims to equip you with the insights and tools necessary to navigate this path with confidence. Whether it's balancing data with intuition, managing risks, or overcoming challenges, the lessons here are designed to empower you to make decisions that propel your business forward.

I am deeply grateful to the CEOs and business leaders who have shared their experiences and wisdom in public media. Their stories are not just about success but also about the trials and tribulations they faced along the way—stories that I hope will inspire and guide you in your own entrepreneurial journey.

Remember, the decisions you make today will shape the future of your enterprise. Embrace the journey, learn from every experience, and trust in your ability to lead. The entrepreneurial spirit is about innovation, perseverance, and the courage to forge new paths.

Thank you for allowing me to be a part of your journey. I hope the insights and stories in this book inspire you to achieve great things.

Warm regards,
Amit Gupta

- *In a world that's changing really quickly, the only strategy that is guaranteed to fail is not taking risks.*

  by Mark Zuckerberg, Facebook:
  Mark Zuckerberg emphasizes the necessity of taking risks in a rapidly evolving environment.

- *It's about making the right decision at the right time and knowing when to take a risk.*

  by Mary Barra, General Motors
  Mary Barra discusses the importance of timing and risk management in decision-making.

- *Don't make decisions based on fear or scarcity. Make them based on what you are aspiring to*

  by Reed Hastings, Netflix:
  Reed Hastings underscores the importance of making aspirational decisions rather than those driven by fear.

CHAPTER ONE

INTRODUCTION

In the intricate and high-stakes world of corporate leadership, decision-making stands as the cornerstone of success. The ability to make informed, timely, and strategic decisions can propel a company to new heights, while missteps can lead to its downfall. Yet, what exactly goes into the decision-making process of a CEO? How do these leaders balance intuition with data, risk with reward, and innovation with stability?

"How CEOs Decide: The Art of Taking Decisions" delves into the minds of some of the most successful and influential CEOs of our time. This book aims to demystify the decision-making process by uncovering the principles, strategies, and mental frameworks that guide these top executives. Through interviews, case studies, and in-depth analysis, we explore the diverse approaches that CEOs employ to navigate complex challenges and seize opportunities.

Understanding the art of decision-making requires examining both the science behind it and the intangible qualities that define great leadership. This book addresses key questions such as how CEOs handle uncertainty, the role of ethics and values in their choices, and the impact of their decisions on stakeholders. Additionally, it sheds light on the importance of self-awareness, emotional intelligence, and the ability to learn from both successes and failures.

By providing a window into the decision-making processes of high-caliber leaders, this book offers invaluable insights for aspiring CEOs, seasoned executives, and anyone interested in the dynamics of leadership. Whether you are looking to refine your own decision-making skills or simply curious about how leaders at the pinnacle of their careers think and act, "How CEOs Decide" serves as a comprehensive guide to mastering the art of taking decisions.

CHAPTER TWO

The Decision-Making Landscape

INTRODUCTION TO DECISION-MAKING

A soft morning light filtered through the expansive windows of the corner office, casting a serene glow over the polished mahogany desk. Seated behind it, Jane Parker, the CEO of a rapidly growing tech company, contemplated the daunting task ahead. Her company was on the brink of a major acquisition, a decision that would either catapult them into the industry's elite or plunge them into unforeseen chaos. The gravity of her choice weighed heavily on her shoulders, a familiar yet always humbling sensation.

Jane had faced countless decisions throughout her career, each one a unique puzzle with its own set of complexities. Yet, she knew that the essence of decision-making remained a constant dance between intuition and analysis. It was a skill honed over years of experience, a blend of art and science that separated the good leaders from the great ones. She thought back to her early days in the industry, when every choice felt like a gamble and every failure a personal defeat.

In those formative years, Jane often sought the counsel of seasoned mentors. She remembered one particular conversation with Robert, a retired CEO known for his impeccable decision-making skills. Over a cup of coffee, Robert had shared a piece of wisdom that stayed with her: "The best decisions come from a place of clarity, not certainty. You will never have all the answers, but you must trust your ability to navigate the unknown."

That advice became a cornerstone of Jane's leadership philosophy. She understood that decision-making was not about eliminating uncertainty but about managing it with confidence and grace. It required a delicate balance of gathering relevant information, assessing risks, and trusting one's instincts. Jane had developed a systematic approach, a mental checklist she ran through whenever faced with a critical choice.

First, she clarified the objective. What was the ultimate goal? Was it growth, stability, innovation, or something else? Understanding the endgame provided a clear direction and prevented her from getting lost in the myriad of details. Next, she gathered data, seeking out quantitative metrics and qualitative insights. Numbers told one part of the story, but the human element—the emotions, motivations, and aspirations of her team and stakeholders—was equally important.

Jane also valued diverse perspectives. She made it a point to consult with her executive team, encouraging open dialogue and constructive debate. Different viewpoints often illuminated aspects of the decision she might have overlooked. This collaborative approach not only enriched her understanding but also fostered a sense of collective ownership over the outcome.

As she sifted through the information and opinions, Jane paid close attention to her gut feelings. Over time, she had learned to trust her intuition, recognizing it as the subconscious synthesis of her experiences and knowledge. It was not infallible, but it often provided a crucial nudge in the right direction.

With the objective clear, data gathered, and perspectives considered, Jane would then assess the risks. She identified potential pitfalls and devised contingency plans, preparing herself and her team for various scenarios. This proactive mindset helped mitigate the fear of the unknown and instilled a sense of preparedness.

In the quiet of her office, Jane took a deep breath, feeling the familiar mix of anticipation and resolve. She knew that the decision she was about to make would shape the future of her company, but she also knew she was ready. It was not about predicting the future with absolute certainty; it was about making the best possible choice with the information at hand, guided by experience, wisdom, and a steadfast belief in her ability to lead.

As she reached for the phone to make the call, Jane felt a sense of calm wash over her. She was not just making a decision; she was crafting the next chapter of her company's story, one thoughtful choice at a time.

THE ROLE OF A CEO

In the heart of every thriving company beats the steady, guiding hand of its CEO. The CEO is not merely an executive; they are the architect of the organization's vision, the custodian of its culture, and the ultimate decision-maker whose choices reverberate through every level of the business. Every decision, no matter how minute, carries the potential to shape the future of the company, making the role both a privilege and a formidable challenge.

A CEO's responsibilities extend far beyond the confines of the boardroom. They are visionaries who must constantly scan the horizon, anticipating market shifts and technological advancements. Their ability to forecast and adapt to change is crucial, as they must navigate the company through the turbulent waters of competition and innovation. This foresight is not merely about predicting trends but also about understanding the underlying forces that drive them and positioning the company to leverage these forces to its advantage.

Leadership, however, is not just about vision; it is about people. A CEO must cultivate a culture that fosters creativity, collaboration, and a shared sense of purpose. This involves more than setting policies or issuing directives. It requires a deep understanding of the human element, the ability to inspire and motivate, and the wisdom to build a team that embodies the company's values and aspirations. The CEO must be both a mentor and a motivator, guiding their team with a blend of empathy and authority.

Decision-making is the crucible in which a CEO's true mettle is tested. These decisions can range from strategic mergers and acquisitions to daily operational choices. Each decision demands a balance of data-driven analysis and intuitive judgment. A CEO must weigh risks and rewards, consider short-term impacts and long-term goals, and remain steadfast in the face of uncertainty. The ability to make informed, decisive choices is what often separates successful leaders from the rest.

Moreover, a CEO must be an effective communicator. They are the voice of the company, both internally and externally. This role requires the ability to articulate the company's vision and strategy clearly and convincingly to employees, investors, and other stakeholders. Transparent communication builds trust, aligns efforts, and galvanizes support even during challenging times. It is through this communication that a CEO can foster a sense of unity and shared purpose across the organization.

Financial acumen is another critical aspect of the CEO's role. They must have a firm grasp of the company's financial health, understanding the intricacies of budgeting, revenue streams, and cost management. This financial stewardship ensures that the company remains solvent and profitable, providing the necessary resources to invest in growth and innovation.

The CEO's role is multifaceted, requiring a delicate balance of vision, leadership, decision-making, communication, and financial management. It is a role that demands resilience, adaptability, and a relentless drive to push the company towards its goals. The weight of the position is immense, but so is the potential for impact. Through their leadership, a CEO not only guides the company but also shapes its legacy, leaving an indelible mark on its journey.

TYPES OF DECISIONS

The conference room was filled with the hum of anticipation. Each member of the executive team was keenly aware that the decisions made today could steer the company in new, uncharted directions. As the CEO looked around the table, the weight of responsibility was palpable. In that moment, the realization hit: not all decisions are created equal. They vary in scope, urgency, and impact. Understanding these nuances is crucial for effective leadership.

Strategic decisions are the bedrock of any organization. These are the high-stakes choices that define the company's long-term trajectory. They involve setting goals, allocating resources, and determining the direction in which the company will grow. For instance, deciding to enter a new market or to acquire a competitor requires a deep understanding of the industry, a keen eye for opportunity, and the courage to take calculated risks. These decisions are often complex and require extensive deliberation, as their outcomes can shape the company's future for years to come.

Operational decisions, on the other hand, are the day-to-day choices that keep the company running smoothly. These decisions are typically more immediate and involve the implementation of strategies already put in place. Whether it's streamlining a production process, managing a supply chain issue, or optimizing workforce efficiency, operational decisions ensure that the company's strategic objectives are met. While they may not carry the same long-term impact as strategic decisions, their importance cannot be underestimated. A misstep in operational decision-making can lead to inefficiencies, increased costs, and ultimately, a loss of competitive advantage.

Tactical decisions fall somewhere in between strategic and operational decisions. They are often short-term in nature but are crucial for achieving strategic goals. These decisions involve the execution of specific tasks or projects that align with the broader strategic plan. For example, launching a marketing campaign to boost a new product's visibility or negotiating a short-term contract with a key supplier are tactical decisions. They require a blend of strategic insight and operational expertise, making them a unique and vital component of the decision-making process.

Another layer to consider is the distinction between programmed and non-programmed decisions. Programmed decisions are routine and repetitive, often governed by established guidelines or policies. These decisions are usually made at lower levels of the organization and are essential for maintaining consistency and efficiency. For example, restocking inventory when it falls below a certain level is a programmed decision.

Non-programmed decisions, in contrast, are novel and unstructured. They require a higher degree of judgment and creativity, as there are no predefined rules to follow. These decisions are typically made by higher-level executives and involve unique situations that demand innovative solutions. For instance, navigating a sudden market disruption or responding to a public relations crisis are non-programmed decisions that test a CEO's ability to think on their feet.

As the discussion in the conference room unfolded, it became clear that a CEO's ability to recognize and adapt to different types of decisions is a hallmark of effective leadership. Whether it's steering the company through long-term strategic shifts, ensuring smooth day-to-day operations, or tackling unexpected challenges, the ability to discern and execute the appropriate type of decision is what sets great leaders apart. Each category of decision-making brings its own set of challenges and opportunities, and mastering them is key to navigating the complex landscape of modern business.

THE IMPORTANCE OF DECISION-MAKING

In the high-stakes world of executive leadership, the weight of every decision a CEO makes reverberates through the entire organization. Each choice is a thread in the intricate tapestry of a company's narrative, influencing not only the immediate outcomes but also the long-term trajectory of the business. For a CEO, the act of decision-making is not merely a task but a profound responsibility that shapes the destiny of the enterprise.

Imagine standing at the helm of a ship navigating through uncharted waters. The horizon is filled with both opportunity and peril, and the course you set determines the fate of everyone on board. This is the perpetual reality for a CEO. The decisions made in the executive suite can propel a company to new heights or steer it into troubled waters. Understanding this, exceptional CEOs cultivate a deep awareness of the gravity of their choices and the ripples they create.

Consider the scenario of a major acquisition. The allure of expanding market share and diversifying product lines can be tantalizing, yet the risks are equally significant. A miscalculation could lead to financial strain, culture clashes, and operational disruptions. Conversely, a well-executed acquisition can unlock synergies, drive growth, and enhance competitive advantage. The CEO must weigh these factors with a blend of analytical rigor and intuitive insight, drawing on both data and experience to navigate the complexities of such a decision

Beyond the strategic implications, decision-making at the CEO level is also a deeply human process. It involves engaging with diverse perspectives, fostering a culture of trust, and empowering teams to contribute their insights. Effective CEOs recognize that they do not hold a monopoly on wisdom. They actively seek out dissenting opinions, understanding that robust debate and critical thinking are essential to refining ideas and avoiding blind spots. This collaborative approach not only strengthens the quality of decisions but also builds a resilient and adaptive organizational culture.

The personal dimension of decision-making cannot be overlooked. Every CEO brings their unique values, experiences, and biases to the table. Self-awareness is crucial; understanding one's own cognitive and emotional tendencies allows for more balanced and objective decision-making. Additionally, the ability to remain calm under pressure, maintain clarity amidst uncertainty, and exhibit the courage to make tough calls are hallmarks of exceptional leadership.

Consider the case of a CEO facing a moral dilemma, such as whether to prioritize short-term profits over long-term sustainability. The decision carries ethical implications that extend beyond the financial bottom line. It touches on the company's reputation, its relationship with stakeholders, and its broader impact on society. Here, the CEO's values and principles play a pivotal role. The courage to make decisions that align with a higher purpose, even in the face of potential backlash, defines true leadership.

In the end, the importance of decision-making for a CEO lies not only in the outcomes but in the process itself. It is about fostering a mindset of continuous learning, embracing complexity, and being willing to adapt in the face of new information. It is about balancing bold vision with prudent risk management, and leading with both head and heart. Through thoughtful and deliberate decision-making, a CEO can guide their organization towards a future that is not just successful but also meaningful and enduring.

CHAPTER THREE

FOUNDATIONS OF EFFECTIVE DECISION-MAKING

COGNITIVE BIASES

In the high-stakes realm of corporate decision-making, cognitive biases often serve as unseen puppeteers, subtly guiding and influencing the choices of even the most seasoned CEOs. These biases, deeply embedded in the human psyche, can shape strategies, dictate responses, and ultimately affect the trajectory of entire organizations. Consider the case of Jonathan, a CEO of a multinational technology firm, who found himself at a crossroads during a crucial merger negotiation.

Jonathan prided himself on his analytical prowess and decision-making acumen. He had built his career on data-driven strategies and meticulous planning. Yet, as he sat in the boardroom, sifting through the details of the proposed merger, he couldn't shake a feeling of unease. Despite all the positive indicators, a nagging doubt lingered. This was not just a matter of numbers; it was a matter of perception.

Unbeknownst to Jonathan, he was grappling with the anchoring bias. The initial valuation presented by the other company had set a mental anchor, influencing his subsequent judgments. Even though his team had conducted thorough due diligence and presented a higher valuation based on tangible assets and future projections, the initial figure still loomed large in his mind. It was as if every piece of data he reviewed was being subconsciously weighed against that first number, skewing his perception and clouding his judgment.

In another boardroom across the city, Emma, the CEO of a leading fashion brand, faced a different challenge. Her company was considering a bold move into sustainable fashion, a rapidly growing market segment. Emma was enthusiastic about the potential, but she couldn't ignore the reservations of her senior executives. Their skepticism was rooted in the status quo bias, a cognitive bias that favors existing conditions over change. The comfort of their current success was a safety net, making the prospect of venturing into uncharted territory seem unnecessarily risky.

Emma's awareness of this bias became her secret weapon. By recognizing that their resistance was not purely based on financial or strategic rationale but was influenced by an inherent preference for familiarity, she was able to address their concerns more effectively. She framed the move not as a radical departure but as an evolution of their brand identity, aligning the new initiative with their core values and long-term vision. This reframing helped her team overcome their initial resistance and embrace the new direction with confidence.

Meanwhile, in the bustling world of startups, Alex, a young CEO of a burgeoning fintech company, faced a classic example of confirmation bias. Eager to secure venture capital, he had become fixated on data that supported his optimistic projections while dismissing any evidence to the contrary. His pitch meetings were filled with charts and graphs that painted a rosy picture, but they lacked the balance that investors sought.

A mentor's intervention proved to be a turning point for Alex. By challenging him to critically evaluate his assumptions and consider alternative scenarios, Alex learned to present a more balanced and credible case. This shift not only improved his chances of securing funding but also instilled a more rigorous and objective approach to his decision-making process.

These stories underscore the profound impact of cognitive biases on executive decisions. Whether it's the subtle influence of anchoring, the comforting allure of the status quo, or the selective vision of confirmation bias, these mental shortcuts can lead even the most rational leaders astray. Recognizing and mitigating these biases is not just a psychological exercise; it's a strategic imperative for any CEO aiming to navigate the complex landscape of modern business.

EMOTIONAL INTELLIGENCE

In the bustling corridors of corporate power, where decisions ripple through the fabric of entire industries, there exists an invisible yet potent force shaping the fate of enterprises. It is not merely the cold calculus of spreadsheets or the strategic prowess of seasoned executives. It is a deeper, more nuanced attribute that separates the great leaders from the good ones.

In the boardroom of a multinational conglomerate, the conversation had taken an unexpected turn. The quarterly reports were promising, yet the atmosphere was thick with unspoken tension. The CEO, a figure known for his sharp intellect and steely resolve, sensed the undercurrents of unease. Instead of pressing forward with his agenda, he paused, scanning the faces around the table. Each executive was a master of their domain, yet something intangible weighed on their collective psyche.

He leaned back, allowing a moment of silence to permeate the room. "Is there something we're not addressing?" he asked, his voice neither commanding nor dismissive, but genuinely inquisitive. The question hung in the air, an invitation rather than an interrogation. Slowly, one of the senior VPs spoke up, voicing concerns that had been festering beneath the surface. Others followed, and soon the room was alive with a candid, if uncomfortable, dialogue.

This CEO understood something fundamental: the power of emotional intelligence. It was not just about recognizing and managing his own emotions, but about cultivating an environment where others felt safe to express theirs. This skill, often overshadowed by more tangible metrics of success, proved to be a cornerstone of effective leadership.

Emotional intelligence, or EQ, encompasses a range of competencies, from self-awareness to empathy, that enable leaders to navigate the complexities of human dynamics. In the high-stakes world of corporate decision-making, these skills become invaluable. A CEO with high EQ can discern the unspoken fears and motivations of their team, leveraging this insight to foster collaboration and drive innovation.

Consider another scenario: a tech startup on the brink of a major product launch. The pressure is immense, the stakes astronomical. The CEO, a visionary with a penchant for disruptive ideas, notices that her team is on edge, their usual camaraderie fraying under the strain. Instead of pushing harder, she calls for a team retreat. It's not a frivolous escape, but a strategic move to recalibrate their collective mindset.

During the retreat, she shares her own anxieties about the launch, creating a space where vulnerability is not a weakness but a strength. Her openness encourages others to share their own fears and hopes, transforming the team's dynamic. They return not just recharged, but more cohesive, their shared emotional landscape now a foundation for their collective success.

These anecdotes highlight a critical truth: the most effective CEOs are not those who distance themselves from the emotional currents of their organizations, but those who engage with them. They recognize that emotions are not distractions but data points, integral to understanding the human elements that drive business outcomes.

In the labyrinthine world of corporate leadership, where every decision carries weight, emotional intelligence serves as a compass. It guides leaders through the complexities of human interaction, enabling them to make decisions that are not only strategic but also resonant with the values and aspirations of their teams. It is this blend of intellect and empathy that defines the exceptional CEO, one who not only charts the course but also inspires those who follow.

RISK ASSESSMENT

The boardroom was quiet, the kind of silence that follows a high-stakes question. Every eye turned to the CEO, waiting for his decision. He leaned back in his chair, fingers steepled, eyes scanning the room. The air was thick with anticipation, each executive aware that the future of the company hung in the balance. This was the moment that separated great leaders from the rest: the ability to assess risk with precision and confidence.

For a CEO, risk isn't an abstract concept confined to financial spreadsheets or market forecasts. It's a living, breathing entity that weaves itself into every decision, every strategic pivot. The ability to evaluate risk is less about avoiding it and more about understanding its contours, its potential impacts, and its hidden opportunities. This is where intuition meets analysis, where experience melds with data.

The CEO knows that risk is multifaceted. It can be market-driven, stemming from economic downturns or disruptive technologies. It can be operational, emerging from supply chain vulnerabilities or talent shortages. Regulatory changes, geopolitical tensions, and even environmental factors add layers of complexity. The question isn't whether risks exist but how they are navigated and leveraged

He recalls an instance from a few years ago. The company was poised to enter an emerging market with enormous potential but also significant uncertainties. The data was compelling, yet the risks were palpable. Political instability, currency fluctuations, and cultural differences loomed large. The leadership team was divided, some advocating for caution, others urging boldness. The CEO's decision-making process became a masterclass in risk assessment.

He began by dissecting the risks, breaking them down into manageable components. What were the worst-case scenarios? How could they be mitigated? He sought insights from diverse perspectives, engaging not just the executive team but also frontline employees, local experts, and even competitors. Each viewpoint added a layer of understanding, transforming abstract fears into concrete challenges.

He balanced quantitative analysis with qualitative insights. Financial models projected various outcomes, stress-tested against different scenarios. But numbers alone couldn't capture the nuances of local market dynamics or the resilience of the company's operational capabilities. Here, the CEO's intuition, honed by years of experience, played a crucial role. He sensed patterns, identified blind spots, and weighed intangible factors that eluded spreadsheets.

The CEO also recognized the importance of timing. Risk is fluid, its profile shifting with external events and internal developments. He didn't rush to a decision but instead allowed the situation to unfold, gathering more data and refining his assessment. This patience wasn't indecision but strategic prudence, ensuring that when the moment came, the decision would be both informed and timely.

Communication was another critical element. The CEO ensured that the rationale behind the decision was transparent, aligning the team around a shared vision. He articulated the risks and the strategies to address them, fostering a culture of trust and accountability. This wasn't about assuaging fears but about empowering the team to navigate uncertainties with confidence and clarity.

Ultimately, the CEO decided to proceed with the market entry, but with a phased approach that allowed for adjustments based on real-time feedback. The risks were managed, not eliminated, and the company thrived in the new market, reaping rewards that far outweighed the initial fears.

In these moments, the CEO's role transcends traditional leadership. It becomes an art, a delicate balance of courage and caution, vision and vigilance. The ability to assess risk isn't just a skill but a mindset, a way of seeing the world not as a series of threats but as a landscape of possibilities. And in that landscape, true leaders don't just survive; they thrive.

ETHICAL CONSIDERATIONS

In the hushed corridors of corporate power, decisions are often made that ripple far beyond the confines of the boardroom. As CEOs navigate the labyrinth of choices, the compass they wield isn't just forged from strategy and data, but also from the nuanced realm of ethics. The weight of ethical considerations is a silent force, omnipresent and formidable, shaping the decisions that define not just the trajectory of a company, but the very fabric of society.

One might think that ethical dilemmas present themselves with clear demarcations, a simple binary of right and wrong. Yet, in the real-world theatre of business, these dilemmas are often cloaked in ambiguity. Take, for instance, the CEO faced with a decision to cut costs, knowing that the most expedient route involves layoffs. The balance between fiscal responsibility and the well-being of employees becomes a tightrope walk, where each step is laden with moral implications. The decision isn't merely about numbers on a balance sheet but about lives disrupted and communities affected.

In these moments, the personal values of a CEO come to the forefront. The ethical framework they bring into the decision-making process is often a mosaic of their upbringing, experiences, and personal beliefs. A leader who places high value on social responsibility may lean towards solutions that, while potentially more costly, safeguard the interests of their employees and the community. Conversely, a CEO whose ethical compass is guided by shareholder value might prioritize financial efficiency, even at the expense of human capital. Herein lies the crux of ethical decision-making: the inherent tension between competing values and the necessity to reconcile them in a way that aligns with both personal integrity and corporate goals.

Moreover, the role of transparency cannot be overstated. Ethical decision-making thrives in an environment where transparency is not just a policy but a practice. CEOs who foster a culture of openness, where stakeholders are informed and engaged, often find themselves better equipped to navigate ethical quandaries. Transparency builds trust, and with trust comes the latitude to make difficult decisions with the assurance that stakeholders understand the underlying principles guiding those choices.

Yet, transparency alone is not a panacea. The ethical landscape is also shaped by the broader societal context in which a company operates. Social norms, legal frameworks, and cultural expectations all play pivotal roles in defining what is considered ethical. A CEO must be attuned to these external factors, understanding that ethical decision-making is not conducted in a vacuum but is intrinsically linked to the broader societal fabric. This awareness requires a constant recalibration of ethical standards, ensuring that they remain relevant and responsive to an ever-evolving world.

The interplay between personal ethics and corporate responsibility creates a dynamic tension that can be both challenging and enriching. For a CEO, the ability to navigate this terrain is not merely a function of intellectual acumen but of moral fortitude. It demands a willingness to confront uncomfortable truths, to question deeply held beliefs, and to make decisions that, while not always popular, are grounded in a commitment to doing what is right.

In the end, the ethical considerations that underlie a CEO's decisions are a testament to their character. They reflect a deeper understanding that the true measure of leadership is not just in the outcomes achieved but in the integrity with which those outcomes are pursued. The decisions made in the quiet solitude of a CEO's office resonate far beyond the immediate horizon, echoing through the lives of employees, the health of communities, and the conscience of society.

CHAPTER FOUR

STRATEGIC THINKING

LONG-TERM VISION

In the dimly lit boardroom of a towering skyscraper, the atmosphere was thick with anticipation. The CEO, a figure of quiet authority, took his place at the head of the table, his eyes scanning the faces of his trusted advisors. He understood that the decisions made in this room would shape the future of the company for decades to come. It wasn't just about the next quarter or the annual report; it was about casting a vision that would guide the organization through the shifting tides of the global market.

He began to speak, his voice steady and measured. He spoke of the importance of seeing beyond the immediate horizon, of imagining a future that others could not yet conceive. It was not enough to react to changes as they came; true leadership required the ability to anticipate them, to position the company in a place of strength before the waves of change crashed upon the shore.

The CEO shared stories of leaders who had failed to look beyond their immediate surroundings. Companies that had once been titans of their industries, now reduced to footnotes in history books. He spoke of the dangers of short-term thinking, of the seductive allure of quick wins that ultimately led to long-term losses. His words were a stark reminder that the path to lasting success was not paved with easy choices.

As he spoke, he painted a picture of a future where the company not only survived but thrived. He described new markets to be explored, innovative products yet to be developed, and strategic partnerships that could open doors to unprecedented opportunities. His vision was not just a dream; it was a carefully crafted blueprint, built on a foundation of research, data, and a deep understanding of the industry.

Around the table, the advisors listened intently. They knew that the CEO's vision would require more than just their intellectual buy-in; it would demand their unwavering commitment, their willingness to take calculated risks, and their ability to inspire their teams to rally behind a common goal. They understood that true leadership was not about dictating orders but about fostering a shared sense of purpose.

The CEO's vision extended beyond the company itself. He spoke of the broader impact they could have on society, of their responsibility to not only generate profits but to do so in a way that was sustainable and ethical. He envisioned a future where the company was a leader in corporate social responsibility, setting standards that others would aspire to follow.

As the meeting drew to a close, the CEO looked around the room, his gaze meeting each advisor's eyes. He knew that the road ahead would be fraught with challenges, that there would be moments of doubt and uncertainty. But he also knew that with a clear vision, a dedicated team, and a commitment to excellence, they could navigate the complexities of the business world and emerge stronger on the other side.

The advisors left the boardroom with a renewed sense of purpose. They carried with them the CEO's vision, ready to translate it into actionable strategies and concrete results. They understood that their decisions today would shape the legacy of the company for generations to come. And as they stepped into the future, they did so with the confidence that they were not just following a leader, but becoming leaders themselves.

SWOT ANALYSIS

The boardroom was alive with anticipation as the senior leadership team gathered around the expansive mahogany table. The air was thick with the weight of the decisions that lay ahead. Jonathan, the seasoned CEO of a multinational conglomerate, leaned forward, his eyes scanning the room. It was time to dissect the company's current standing and chart a course for the future. He knew that a structured approach was essential, and today, they would delve into the intricate process of a SWOT analysis.

SWOT—Strengths, Weaknesses, Opportunities, Threats. Four words that held the key to unlocking actionable insights about the company. Jonathan began by addressing the strengths. The company had a well-established brand reputation, a diverse and skilled workforce, and a strong financial position. These assets were the backbone of their competitive advantage. He emphasized the importance of leveraging these strengths to maintain their market position and drive growth.

The conversation then shifted to weaknesses. It was a moment of introspection, where vulnerabilities were laid bare. The company's over-reliance on a few key markets and products, the slow adoption of new technologies, and the bureaucratic layers that stifled innovation were highlighted. Jonathan encouraged an open dialogue, urging his team to confront these issues head-on. Acknowledging weaknesses was not a sign of defeat, but a step towards transformation.

Opportunities were the next focal point. The world was evolving rapidly, and with change came potential. Emerging markets, advancements in technology, and shifting consumer behaviors presented a plethora of possibilities. Jonathan's eyes sparkled with excitement as he spoke of expanding into new territories, investing in digital transformation, and developing sustainable products. The room buzzed with a renewed sense of purpose, as the team brainstormed ways to capitalize on these opportunities.

The discussion took a somber turn as they examined threats. The competitive landscape was fierce, with new entrants disrupting the market. Economic instability, regulatory changes, and the looming threat of cybersecurity breaches added to the complexity. Jonathan's tone was resolute as he articulated the need for vigilance and proactive measures. Understanding these threats was crucial for developing robust risk management strategies.

Throughout the session, Jonathan's leadership shone through. He navigated the conversation with finesse, balancing optimism with realism. The SWOT analysis was not just a theoretical exercise; it was a dynamic tool that guided decision-making. It provided a comprehensive view of the internal and external factors influencing the company. By systematically analyzing each component, the team could prioritize actions and allocate resources effectively.

As the meeting drew to a close, the room was filled with a sense of clarity and determination. The SWOT analysis had illuminated the path forward. Jonathan knew that the real work was just beginning. The insights gained today would inform strategic planning, drive innovation, and foster resilience. The company was well-equipped to navigate the complexities of the business world.

In the days that followed, the leadership team translated the SWOT analysis into a strategic roadmap. Initiatives were launched to strengthen core capabilities, mitigate weaknesses, seize opportunities, and counteract threats. Jonathan's decision-making process, grounded in the principles of SWOT, exemplified how CEOs could steer their organizations towards sustained success.

The art of decision-making was nuanced, requiring a blend of analytical rigor and visionary thinking. Jonathan's approach demonstrated that understanding the intricacies of one's environment, both internal and external, was essential for making informed and impactful choices. The SWOT analysis was not just a tool, but a testament to the power of strategic insight in the hands of a decisive leader.

SCENARIO PLANNING

In the bustling heart of a major tech corporation, CEO Richard Mann sat in his glass-walled office, contemplating the myriad paths his company could take. The world outside was ever-changing, and the future seemed more uncertain than ever. He knew that to steer his company through these turbulent waters, he needed more than just intuition and experience. He required a structured approach to foresee potential challenges and opportunities. Richard turned his thoughts to scenario planning, a tool he had learned about during a leadership seminar years ago.

Richard recalled the seminar vividly. The speaker, a seasoned strategist, had painted a picture of a volatile business environment where traditional forecasting methods often fell short. Scenario planning, he had explained, was about preparing for multiple, plausible futures rather than attempting to predict a single outcome. It was a method that allowed leaders to anticipate a range of possibilities, identify potential risks, and develop strategic responses.

With this in mind, Richard called a meeting with his senior leadership team. Around the table sat his trusted advisors: Jenna, the CFO with a knack for numbers and risk management; Carlos, the COO who excelled in operational efficiency; and Priya, the CMO who had a finger on the pulse of market trends and consumer behavior. Richard outlined his vision for scenario planning and tasked each of them with contributing their expertise.

The team began by identifying key drivers of change in their industry. They considered technological advancements, regulatory shifts, economic fluctuations, and social trends. Each driver was analyzed for its potential impact on the company, both positive and negative. The room buzzed with ideas as they brainstormed various scenarios, from best-case to worst-case, and everything in between.

One scenario envisioned a rapid technological breakthrough that could render their current product line obsolete. Another imagined a severe economic downturn that would drastically reduce consumer spending. They also considered a scenario where new regulations imposed stringent requirements on their operations. Each scenario was fleshed out with detailed narratives, outlining the sequence of events and the resulting implications for the company.

As they delved deeper, the team began to see patterns and connections between different drivers and scenarios. They identified key uncertainties that could have a significant impact on their business, such as the pace of technological change and the stability of global markets. These uncertainties became the focal points of their scenario planning efforts.

With the scenarios mapped out, the team turned their attention to developing strategic responses. For each scenario, they outlined potential actions the company could take to mitigate risks and seize opportunities. They considered diversifying their product line, investing in research and development, and strengthening their financial reserves. They also discussed ways to enhance their agility, so they could quickly adapt to changing circumstances.

Richard felt a sense of clarity and preparedness as the team presented their findings. The scenarios provided a framework for thinking about the future in a structured way, allowing the company to be proactive rather than reactive. While they couldn't predict exactly what would happen, they were now equipped with a range of strategies to navigate the uncertainties ahead.

The exercise also fostered a culture of collaboration and forward-thinking within the leadership team. It encouraged open dialogue and diverse perspectives, which Richard knew were crucial for effective decision-making. As the meeting concluded, he felt confident that they had taken an important step towards securing the company's future.

Richard leaned back in his chair, satisfied with the progress they had made. Scenario planning had not only given them a roadmap for the future but also strengthened their resolve to face whatever challenges lay ahead.

RESOURCE ALLOCATION

In the bustling heart of a thriving metropolis, the corner office of the CEO was not just a vantage point; it was a crucible where decisions forged the future. The CEO, a figure of quiet intensity, often found themselves at the crossroads of opportunity and constraint. The art and science of resource allocation was a dance that required not just precision but a deep understanding of the company's pulse.

Every morning, the CEO would review the latest reports, a tapestry of numbers and narratives that painted the current state of the business. Each department, from marketing to R&D, clamored for a slice of the finite budget. The challenge was not merely to distribute resources but to do so in a way that aligned with the company's long-term vision and immediate needs.

The CEO knew that resource allocation was about more than just money. It was about time, talent, and attention. One of the most critical decisions was where to direct the company's brightest minds. The CEO had learned through experience that the right team, focused on the right project, could turn a modest investment into a substantial return. Conversely, even a generous budget could be squandered if not paired with the right people and priorities.

In one particularly memorable instance, the CEO faced a dilemma. Two promising projects were vying for resources: one, an innovative product that had the potential to disrupt the market; the other, an upgrade to an existing product line that promised steady, reliable revenue. The board was divided, each side presenting compelling arguments. The CEO, however, looked beyond the immediate numbers. They considered the company's core strengths, market trends, and the long-term strategic goals. In a decisive move, the CEO allocated the majority of resources to the innovative product, believing that the risk was justified by the potential for significant market impact.

This decision was not made lightly. The CEO had spent countless hours discussing with the heads of R&D, marketing, and finance. They listened to the concerns and aspirations of the team, weighing the potential risks and rewards. The CEO knew that successful resource allocation required a balance of intuition and analysis, a willingness to take calculated risks, and the foresight to anticipate future needs.

The CEO also understood the importance of flexibility. Markets could shift, new opportunities could arise, and unforeseen challenges could emerge. The ability to reallocate resources swiftly and effectively was crucial. The CEO had established a culture of agility within the company, encouraging departments to remain adaptable and responsive to change. This approach allowed the company to pivot when necessary, ensuring that resources were always directed where they could have the most significant impact.

One of the CEO's most valuable tools was a robust feedback loop. Regular reviews and open communication channels ensured that the CEO was always informed about the progress and challenges of various projects. This feedback allowed for timely adjustments, preventing small issues from escalating into major problems. It also fostered a sense of shared responsibility and collaboration among the team, reinforcing the idea that resource allocation was a collective endeavor.

Through these experiences, the CEO had come to view resource allocation as a dynamic, ongoing process rather than a one-time decision. It was an intricate balancing act that required constant vigilance, strategic foresight, and a deep understanding of the company's evolving landscape. In the end, it was this nuanced approach that enabled the CEO to steer the company towards sustained growth and innovation, ensuring that every resource was invested with purpose and precision.

CHAPTER FIVE

DATA-DRIVEN DECISIONS

IMPORTANCE OF DATA

Data whispered its importance in quiet, unassuming ways. For CEOs, those whispers often became a chorus, impossible to ignore. In the boardrooms and private offices where decisions shape the future of companies, data stood as an unyielding sentinel, guiding every move, every strategy. Its significance was not just in the numbers, but in the stories it told, the insights it revealed, and the paths it illuminated.

In the early days of any business, intuition and experience might carry the weight. There's a certain charm in the gut feeling of a seasoned leader, the kind of instinct honed over years of navigating markets and managing crises. However, as companies grow, the stakes rise, and the complexity of decisions multiplies. It's here that data transforms from a helpful tool to an indispensable asset.

Imagine a CEO pondering the launch of a new product. The potential rewards are vast—new markets, increased revenue, enhanced brand reputation. But the risks are equally daunting. A misstep could mean millions lost, reputations tarnished, and opportunities squandered. It is in this crucible of decision-making that data reveals its true power. Market research, consumer behavior analytics, and financial projections come together to paint a picture that instinct alone could never capture.

In the hands of a skilled leader, data becomes more than just raw numbers. It's a narrative of customer needs, a map of market trends, a forecast of financial outcomes. CEOs who understand this wield data like a master craftsman uses their tools—precisely, strategically, and with a clear vision of the outcome. They know that each data point is a piece of a larger puzzle, and only by seeing the whole picture can they make decisions that steer their companies toward success.

Consider the story of a tech startup on the brink of a major pivot. The CEO, faced with declining user engagement and stagnant growth, turned to data for answers. By diving deep into user analytics, market trends, and competitive landscapes, they uncovered insights that were not immediately apparent. Perhaps it was a shift in consumer preferences, a gap in the market that their current offerings didn't fill, or a new technology that could revolutionize their product. Armed with this knowledge, the CEO could make informed decisions about where to focus resources, how to adapt their strategy, and what innovations to pursue.

Data also plays a crucial role in risk management. In an era where volatility is the norm, understanding and mitigating risks is as important as seizing opportunities. For a CEO, data provides a detailed risk assessment, highlighting potential pitfalls and enabling proactive measures. Whether it's economic indicators signaling a downturn, or social media sentiment hinting at a PR crisis, being forewarned is being forearmed.

In the world of mergers and acquisitions, data's role is even more pronounced. Due diligence, market valuations, and synergy assessments hinge on accurate, comprehensive data. A CEO equipped with the right information can negotiate better deals, foresee integration challenges, and ultimately, make decisions that add real value to their company.

In every sector, from healthcare to finance, from retail to manufacturing, data's importance is a constant. It's the foundation upon which modern business decisions are built. For CEOs, understanding its value and harnessing its power is not just beneficial—it's essential. In the rapidly evolving landscape of today's business world, those who master data will lead, while those who ignore it risk being left behind.

DATA COLLECTION METHODS

In the quest to understand the decision-making processes of CEOs, the journey of data collection is as critical as the insights it aims to uncover. The book delves into the intricate tapestry of methods employed to gather comprehensive, accurate, and actionable data. It is not merely about numbers and statistics; it is about capturing the essence of leadership, the nuances of choices, and the subtleties of executive rationale.

A multifaceted approach is essential to paint a holistic picture of how CEOs decide. Interviews stand as a cornerstone in this endeavor. Engaging directly with CEOs, these conversations reveal the intricacies of their thought processes, strategies, and the internal and external factors influencing their decisions. Interviews are conducted in a manner that fosters openness and honesty, encouraging leaders to share not just their successes but also their missteps and the lessons learned from them.

Surveys complement these interviews, offering a broader quantitative perspective. Carefully crafted questionnaires are distributed to a wider pool of CEOs, capturing data on common patterns, trends, and deviations in decision-making. The responses provide a statistical backbone to the qualitative insights gleaned from interviews, allowing for a more comprehensive understanding of the landscape.

Case studies offer another layer of depth. By examining specific instances of decision-making within various companies, these studies provide context-rich insights into the challenges faced by CEOs and the strategies they employ. Each case study is meticulously documented, highlighting the situational variables, the decision-making process, the outcomes, and the subsequent reflections of the CEOs involved. These real-world examples serve as invaluable learning tools, illustrating the complexities and dynamism of executive decisions.

Observations also play a critical role. By immersing in the daily environments of CEOs, researchers can witness firsthand the dynamics of leadership and decision-making in action. This method allows for the capture of non-verbal cues, spontaneous reactions, and the real-time interplay between CEOs and their teams. Such observations are instrumental in understanding the practical application of theoretical concepts and the real-world constraints and pressures that shape decisions.

Document analysis provides another vital piece of the puzzle. By reviewing internal memos, strategic plans, meeting minutes, and other relevant documents, researchers can trace the evolution of decisions and the rationale behind them. This method offers a retrospective view, allowing for the identification of patterns and the assessment of decision-making effectiveness over time.

Engaging with stakeholders—such as board members, senior executives, and employees—adds another dimension to the data collection process. These perspectives provide a more rounded view of the CEO's decision-making environment and the ripple effects of their choices. Understanding the perceptions and reactions of those directly impacted by executive decisions enriches the overall analysis.

Triangulation of these methods ensures the robustness of the data. By cross-referencing findings from interviews, surveys, case studies, observations, document analysis, and stakeholder engagements, the research mitigates biases and enhances the reliability of the conclusions drawn. This comprehensive approach ensures that the insights presented are not only accurate but also reflective of the multifaceted nature of CEO decision-making.

The meticulous process of data collection is not just a means to an end but an integral part of understanding how CEOs navigate the complexities of leadership. Each method, with its unique strengths and perspectives, contributes to a richer, more nuanced understanding of the art and science of executive decision-making.

ANALYZING DATA

In the quiet solitude of a CEO's office, amidst the hum of computers and the soft rustle of papers, lies a moment of profound contemplation. Before decisions can be made, data must be understood. The journey into the labyrinth of numbers, charts, and trends is not just a task but an art form, demanding both intuition and intellect.

The room is filled with the scent of coffee and the soft glow of a desk lamp. A CEO sits at the helm, surrounded by reports, each one a potential key to unlocking the future of the company. The data sprawls out like an intricate tapestry, each thread representing a different aspect of the business. Sales figures from the last quarter, customer feedback scores, market trends, and financial forecasts—all these elements demand attention.

The first step is immersion. The CEO dives deep into the data, not just skimming the surface but swimming through the depths. Numbers are not merely digits on a page; they are stories waiting to be told. Each percentage point in a sales report could signify a triumph or a challenge. A sudden spike in customer complaints might reveal a deeper issue within the product line. As the CEO reads, patterns begin to emerge, like constellations in the night sky. These patterns are the first whispers of insight.

But data alone is not enough. It must be contextualized. The CEO thinks back to recent board meetings, recalls conversations with department heads, and considers the broader economic landscape. This context transforms raw data into meaningful information. A dip in sales might be alarming, but if it coincides with a seasonal trend, it might not be as dire as it seems. The CEO's experience and knowledge act as a lens, bringing the data into sharper focus.

Next comes the synthesis. The CEO begins to weave together disparate pieces of information, creating a coherent narrative. This is where intuition plays a crucial role. It's not just about what the data says, but what it implies. A sudden increase in website traffic, paired with a drop in conversion rates, might suggest a problem with the user experience. The CEO's mind races, considering possibilities and implications, forming hypotheses that must be tested.

Collaboration is the next critical element. The CEO reaches out to trusted advisors, data analysts, and department heads. Together, they dissect the data, challenging assumptions and validating findings. This collaborative effort ensures that the insights are robust and reliable. Different perspectives bring new dimensions to the analysis, uncovering nuances that might have been overlooked.

Finally, the CEO must make sense of the insights gained. This involves not just understanding what the data says, but what it means for the company's future. Strategic decisions are crafted based on these insights. Should the company pivot its product strategy? Is there a need for a marketing overhaul? Are there opportunities for cost savings or new revenue streams? Each decision is a thread that will shape the future tapestry of the company.

In this quiet moment of analysis, the CEO is not just interpreting data but envisioning the future. The decisions made here will ripple out, affecting employees, customers, and stakeholders. The weight of responsibility is immense, but so is the potential for impact. Through careful analysis, informed by experience and enriched by collaboration, the CEO navigates the complex landscape of data, charting a course for success.

MAKING DECISIONS BASED ON DATA

As the sun dipped below the horizon, casting long shadows across the boardroom, Eleanor sat at the head of the table, her eyes scanning the faces of her executive team. The air was thick with anticipation; a critical decision loomed on the horizon. Eleanor had always prided herself on her intuition, but tonight, she felt the weight of the company's future pressing down on her shoulders. The stakes were higher than ever before, and she knew that relying solely on gut feelings would not suffice.

She turned her gaze to the screen at the end of the room, where a series of charts and graphs illuminated the space. Data. Cold, hard numbers that told a story more complex than any novel. Eleanor had come to realize that in the modern business world, decisions grounded in data were not just advantageous; they were essential. The era of making choices based on hunches and instincts was fading, replaced by a new paradigm where data reigned supreme.

Her CTO, Marcus, began to speak, his voice steady and confident. He presented a detailed analysis of the company's recent performance metrics, market trends, and customer behavior patterns. Each data point was meticulously crafted, painting a picture of where the company stood and where it could go. Eleanor listened intently, her mind racing to connect the dots. She had seen the power of data-driven decisions before, but never on such a grand scale.

As the presentation continued, Eleanor's thoughts drifted to a conversation she had with a fellow CEO at a conference months prior. The CEO had shared a story about a pivotal moment in his career when he had to choose between two seemingly equal paths. It was the data that had tipped the scales, revealing insights he would have otherwise overlooked. That decision had propelled his company to unprecedented success. Eleanor had been skeptical at the time, but now she understood. Data was not just a tool; it was a compass, guiding leaders through the fog of uncertainty.

When Marcus finished, the room fell silent. All eyes were on Eleanor, waiting for her to speak. She took a deep breath, feeling the enormity of the moment. The data presented was compelling, but it was not just about the numbers. It was about interpreting them, understanding their implications, and making a choice that would steer the company in the right direction.

Eleanor leaned forward, her fingers tapping lightly on the table. "Thank you, Marcus," she said, her voice clear and resolute. "The data you've presented is invaluable. It provides us with a clear picture of our current state and potential future. However, we must also consider the human element. Data can guide us, but it cannot replace our judgment and experience."

She paused, letting her words sink in. "We will use this data to inform our decision, but we must also trust in our collective wisdom. Together, we will analyze the numbers, weigh the risks, and choose the path that aligns with our vision and values."

The room buzzed with renewed energy as her team began to discuss the data, their voices rising and falling in a symphony of ideas and insights. Eleanor felt a sense of clarity and determination. She knew that by combining the power of data with the intuition and experience of her team, they could navigate the challenges ahead and lead the company to new heights.

As the discussion continued, Eleanor couldn't help but smile. She had always believed in the strength of her team, and now, fortified by the insights gleaned from the data, she felt more confident than ever in their ability to make the right decisions. The future was uncertain, but with data as their guide, they were ready to face whatever lay ahead.

CHAPTER SIX

THE ROLE OF INTUITION

UNDERSTANDING INTUITION

Sitting in his glass-walled office overlooking the bustling cityscape, Jacob had always believed in the power of data. He surrounded himself with numbers, charts, and reports that provided a semblance of predictability in the chaotic world of business. Yet, there was a part of him that he could never fully quantify, a whispering voice that often nudged him toward decisions that defied pure logic.

It was during a particularly tumultuous quarter that Jacob first began to truly appreciate this enigmatic force. The market was volatile, and his board of directors was split on whether to pivot the company's strategy or stay the course. The data was inconclusive, and every analytical tool at his disposal seemed to offer a different narrative. Amid the cacophony of opinions and projections, Jacob found himself drifting back to a memory from his early career.

Years ago, as a young entrepreneur, he had faced a similar crossroads. His fledgling startup was on the brink of collapse, and every advisor he consulted recommended shutting down. But something inside him resisted. It wasn't stubbornness or blind optimism; it was a deeply rooted sense that he was on the verge of a breakthrough. Against all advice, he decided to push forward. That decision, driven by a gut feeling, had eventually led him to the success he enjoyed today.

Jacob realized that what he had experienced was not mere happenstance. It was intuition—a form of intelligence that transcended conventional analysis. He began to see intuition as a crucial tool in his decision-making arsenal, one that could complement, rather than contradict, data-driven insights.

Intrigued by this revelation, Jacob started to explore the concept of intuition more deeply. He read about how renowned CEOs like Steve Jobs and Richard Branson often credited their success to intuitive decisions. He learned about the science behind it, how the brain processes vast amounts of information subconsciously, drawing on past experiences and patterns to generate intuitive hunches.

One evening, Jacob attended a lecture by a renowned psychologist specializing in decision-making. The psychologist spoke about the "adaptive unconscious," a term that described the brain's ability to make quick, yet highly informed decisions without conscious deliberation. Jacob was fascinated by the idea that intuition was not some mystical force but a sophisticated cognitive process honed by years of experience and learning.

Inspired, he decided to put this newfound understanding to the test. During the next board meeting, as his team debated the company's direction, Jacob listened intently to their analyses but also paid attention to his own intuitive responses. When the moment came to make a decision, he found himself leaning towards a path that the data alone did not fully support. It was a risky move, but his intuition told him it was the right one.

Months later, the decision proved to be a turning point for the company. The pivot led to new opportunities and growth that none of the data models had predicted. Jacob's faith in intuition had been vindicated.

As he reflected on this journey, Jacob understood that being a successful CEO required more than just analytical prowess. It demanded a balance between the tangible and the intangible, the measurable and the immeasurable. Through this balance, he found a deeper sense of clarity and confidence in his leadership, realizing that intuition was not the antithesis of reason but its powerful ally.

BALANCING INTUITION AND DATA

As the sun dipped below the horizon, casting long shadows across the cityscape, Eleanor sat in her corner office, the weight of the upcoming decision pressing on her shoulders. The flickering lights of the skyscrapers outside mirrored the conflicting thoughts racing through her mind. Leading a multinational corporation meant every choice she made reverberated through countless lives and economies. Yet, this particular decision felt different; it was more nuanced, more complex.

Eleanor had always prided herself on her sharp intuition. It was this very instinct that had propelled her from a junior analyst to the CEO's chair in record time. She could sense market shifts before they happened, detect the subtleties in boardroom dynamics, and read between the lines of financial reports. Her gut had rarely led her astray. But now, as she faced a pivotal crossroads, she found herself questioning the reliability of those instincts.

On her desk lay a thick dossier, filled with meticulously gathered data by her team of analysts. Charts, graphs, and projections painted a compelling picture, one that pointed towards a clear course of action. The numbers were persuasive, presenting a logical path forward. However, something gnawed at Eleanor, a whisper in the back of her mind urging caution.

She thought of her mentor, Richard, who had once told her, "Eleanor, the best leaders don't just rely on intuition or data alone. They weave both into a tapestry of informed decision-making." Richard's words echoed in her mind as she paced the room, the soft hum of the city below providing a rhythmic backdrop to her thoughts.

Eleanor approached the window, gazing out at the bustling streets. She remembered a time early in her career when she had ignored a gut feeling in favor of data. The result had been disastrous, leading to a significant financial loss and a bruised confidence. That experience had taught her the importance of balance, of listening to both the heart and the mind.

Returning to her desk, she glanced at the dossier once more. The data was clear, but it lacked the human element, the unpredictable variables that numbers couldn't capture. Her intuition, on the other hand, was shaped by years of experience, by countless interactions and observations. It was a repository of subtle cues and patterns that no algorithm could replicate.

Eleanor decided to call an impromptu meeting with her senior team. She needed their perspectives, their insights to bridge the gap between cold data and warm instinct. As they gathered, she laid out the facts, but also shared her reservations, her gut feelings about potential pitfalls and opportunities.

The discussion was lively, with voices rising and falling, ideas clashing and merging. Her team brought their own blend of intuition and analysis to the table, enriching the conversation. Through their dialogue, a clearer picture began to emerge, one that honored both the empirical evidence and the instinctual hunches.

As the meeting concluded, Eleanor felt a sense of clarity. The path forward was not purely data-driven nor solely based on intuition. It was a harmonious blend of both, a decision that respected the strength of numbers while acknowledging the wisdom of experience.

Eleanor knew that this balance was not a one-time achievement but an ongoing practice, a dynamic equilibrium that required constant attention and adjustment. As she prepared to implement the decision, she felt a renewed confidence. She understood that true leadership lay in the delicate dance between the tangible and the intangible, between the measurable and the immeasurable. And in that dance, she found her stride.

CASE STUDIES IN INTUITIVE DECISIONS

In the bustling heart of Silicon Valley, where innovation meets fierce competition, one CEO stood out not just for his company's success, but for his uncanny ability to make decisions that seemed almost preternatural. Raj Patel, the CEO of TechWave, often found himself in situations where data was scarce, and the stakes were high.

Raj's colleagues marveled at his knack for knowing the right path forward, even when traditional metrics provided no clear guidance. One particularly striking example occurred during the development of a new artificial intelligence platform. The engineering team was divided on whether to pursue a more conservative approach, which would ensure stability but limit innovation, or a radical new design that promised to leapfrog competitors but came with significant risks.

Raj listened intently to both sides, absorbing the technical jargon and weighing the potential outcomes. As the debate intensified, he closed his eyes for a moment, a habit that had become his signature move in times of deep contemplation. When he opened them, he spoke with a calm certainty that cut through the tension. "We go with the radical design," he declared. "It's a risk worth taking." The room fell silent, and then slowly, nods of agreement spread among the team.

The decision paid off spectacularly. TechWave's new platform not only worked but set a new industry standard, catapulting the company ahead of its rivals. Raj later described his decision-making process as a blend of intuition and experience. He had a deep understanding of his industry, but he also trusted his gut, a skill he had honed over years of leading through uncertainty.

Across the globe, in a different industry, another CEO faced a daunting challenge. Maria Gonzalez of GlobaPharm was in the midst of a crisis. A competitor had launched a smear campaign, questioning the safety of one of GlobaPharm's best-selling medications. The board was in a frenzy, and the PR team was scrambling to contain the fallout.

Maria, however, remained composed. She called an emergency meeting and listened to the frantic updates, all the while processing the information with a calm detachment. She then did something unexpected. She instructed her team to halt all defensive press releases and instead focus on gathering and presenting transparent, unequivocal evidence of the medication's safety.

Her decision was rooted in a deep-seated belief in the company's values and the quality of their products. While others might have panicked and gone on the offensive, Maria trusted her intuition, which told her that transparency and integrity would win out. The strategy worked. Public trust in GlobaPharm was restored, and the competitor's campaign backfired, leaving them with a tarnished reputation.

These examples illustrate how CEOs like Raj and Maria leverage intuition in their decision-making processes. Their ability to synthesize information quickly, trust their gut feelings, and make bold choices sets them apart. It's not that they ignore data or analysis; rather, they integrate these elements into a broader framework of intuitive understanding.

In these high-stakes environments, the ability to make swift, confident decisions is invaluable. It's a skill that combines experience, knowledge, and an almost instinctual grasp of what is needed. As we delve deeper into the world of executive decision-making, it becomes clear that intuition plays a pivotal role, guiding leaders through uncharted territories with a sense of clarity that often defies conventional logic.

DEVELOPING INTUITIVE SKILLS

Navigating the labyrinth of executive decision-making often feels like steering a ship through uncharted waters. The compass many CEOs rely on isn't just data or advice from seasoned advisors; it's a finely tuned sense of intuition. This sixth sense, while seemingly mystical, is a skill that can be developed and honed like any other.

Samantha, the CEO of a rapidly growing tech startup, found herself at a crossroads. Her company was on the brink of launching a groundbreaking product, but the market responses during beta testing were mixed. The data was inconclusive, and her team was divided. Samantha had always prided herself on her analytical skills, but this time, the numbers weren't providing a clear direction.

In moments like these, Samantha turned to her intuition. It wasn't a reckless gamble but a decision informed by years of experience, subconscious pattern recognition, and a deep understanding of her industry. She decided to delay the launch by three months to address the feedback and refine the product. It was a risky move, but her gut told her it was the right one. The eventual success of the product vindicated her decision, and she realized that her intuition had been a critical factor.

Developing this intuitive edge isn't about ignoring data or conventional wisdom; it's about integrating them into a broader perspective. For CEOs, this often means stepping back from the noise and creating space for reflection. Regular moments of solitude, whether through daily meditation, long walks, or quiet contemplation, allow the mind to process information at a deeper level.

Tom, the CEO of a manufacturing giant, swore by his morning routine. Each day, before diving into the chaos of meetings and reports, he spent an hour in silence, sipping his coffee and letting his mind wander. This practice, he believed, cleared the mental clutter and allowed his subconscious to surface insights that his conscious mind might overlook. It was during one of these quiet mornings that he had an epiphany about a new market opportunity, something that hadn't been apparent in the data his team had presented.

Another critical aspect is exposure to diverse experiences and perspectives. CEOs who cultivate their intuition often have a breadth of experiences outside their immediate industry. This cross-pollination of ideas helps them see patterns and connections that others might miss. Jane, who leads a global retail chain, made it a point to travel extensively and immerse herself in different cultures. These experiences enriched her understanding of consumer behavior and trends, allowing her to make intuitive leaps that kept her company ahead of the curve.

Trusting one's intuition also requires a certain level of self-awareness and emotional intelligence. CEOs must be attuned to their own biases and emotions, understanding how these can cloud judgment. Regular self-reflection and feedback from trusted advisors help in calibrating this inner compass. Mark, a veteran CEO, often shared his intuitive hunches with his closest confidants, seeking their perspectives to ensure he wasn't being swayed by personal biases or wishful thinking.

In the high-stakes world of executive decision-making, intuition isn't a mystical force but a powerful tool grounded in experience, reflection, and emotional intelligence. CEOs like Samantha, Tom, and Jane demonstrate that by cultivating this skill, leaders can navigate uncertainty with a confidence that data alone cannot provide.

CHAPTER SEVEN

Leadership Styles and Decision-Making

AUTOCRATIC LEADERSHIP

In the dimly lit boardroom, the air was thick with anticipation. Every executive seated around the polished mahogany table knew that today's meeting would be unlike any other. At the head of the table sat Alexander Drake, the enigmatic CEO known for his unyielding grip on the company's helm. His decisions were swift and his authority unquestioned. This was the essence of autocratic leadership, where the power to decide rested solely in the hands of one individual, and Alexander exemplified this style to its core.

Years before, Alexander had taken the reins of a faltering tech company and transformed it into a market leader. His approach was both lauded and criticized, but undeniably effective. He made decisions with a confidence that bordered on audacity, rarely seeking input from his subordinates. For Alexander, the path to success was clear: unwavering control and decisive action.

The executives knew that their role was to execute his vision, not to challenge it. Alexander's leadership style was a double-edged sword. On one hand, it brought about rapid decision-making and clear direction. On the other, it stifled creativity and discouraged open dialogue. Yet, in times of crisis, his methods proved invaluable. When the company faced a critical security breach, Alexander's immediate and unilateral decisions contained the damage and restored customer trust.

Alexander's rise to power was not without its challenges. He had inherited a company mired in bureaucracy and indecision. Meetings were endless, and consensus was elusive. Recognizing the need for a radical shift, Alexander implemented a top-down approach. He streamlined operations, cut through red tape, and established a culture of accountability. His mantra was simple: "Decide and act. Hesitation is the enemy of progress."

His leadership style demanded loyalty and precision. Team members quickly learned that presenting half-baked ideas or uncertain plans was not an option. Alexander expected thorough preparation and unwavering commitment. Those who thrived under his leadership were meticulous and resilient, able to execute his directives with precision.

Despite the apparent rigidity, there was a method to Alexander's madness. He believed that a strong leader must be the anchor in turbulent times. His decisiveness provided a sense of stability in an industry characterized by rapid change and fierce competition. Employees knew where the company was headed and what was expected of them, which, in turn, fostered a disciplined and focused workforce.

However, the cost of such leadership was palpable. Innovation sometimes took a backseat as employees feared the repercussions of presenting unconventional ideas. The atmosphere, though efficient, was often tense. Alexander's presence alone was enough to silence a room, and while this commanded respect, it also bred a culture of compliance over creativity.

As Alexander concluded the meeting, his final words resonated with the clarity and conviction that had become his hallmark. "We move forward with this strategy. No deviations. Execute flawlessly." The executives nodded, understanding the weight of his directive. They knew that under Alexander's autocratic leadership, there was little room for error but ample opportunity for success.

In the world of CEOs, Alexander Drake stood as a testament to the power of autocratic leadership. His reign was characterized by unwavering control, rapid decision-making, and a relentless pursuit of excellence. While his methods were not without flaws, the results spoke for themselves. The company's rise to prominence was a direct reflection of the man at its helm, a leader who decided with unshakable resolve and led with an iron fist.

DEMOCRATIC LEADERSHIP

In the bustling heart of a thriving tech company, CEO Laura had always believed that the strength of her leadership lay in the collective wisdom of her team. Her office was not a secluded corner of the building but a transparent, glass-walled room where anyone could walk in and share their thoughts. Laura had long embraced a leadership style that was less about issuing directives and more about fostering collaboration and inclusivity. Every Monday morning, the entire company would gather in the open-plan workspace for a meeting that was anything but ordinary.

At these meetings, Laura didn't stand at the head of the room to deliver a monologue. Instead, she sat among her team members, encouraging open dialogue and participation. She understood that the best ideas often came from the most unexpected places. One such Monday, the conversation veered towards a looming challenge: the launch of a new product line that had the potential to redefine the company's market position. The stakes were high, and the room buzzed with a mix of excitement and apprehension.

Laura initiated the discussion by presenting the core idea and the challenges they faced. Instead of dictating the next steps, she turned to her team and asked, "What do you all think?" This simple question opened the floodgates of creativity. Engineers, marketers, and customer service representatives all contributed their perspectives. The engineers discussed technical feasibility, the marketers explored potential market reception, and the customer service team highlighted possible user concerns.

As the conversation unfolded, Laura skillfully guided it, ensuring that every voice was heard. She was not just a participant but a facilitator, weaving together the diverse threads of input into a cohesive strategy. Her approach was grounded in the belief that when people felt valued and heard, they were more invested in the outcome. This was not just a theoretical stance; it was a practical strategy that had consistently driven the company's success.

The democratic nature of these meetings did not mean that decisions were made by consensus alone. Laura knew that leadership sometimes required making tough calls. However, by involving her team in the decision-making process, she ensured that when those calls had to be made, they were well-informed and had the buy-in of the majority. This approach built a culture of trust and mutual respect, where employees felt empowered to take initiative and innovate.

One of the most memorable instances of this leadership style in action was during the development of their flagship product. The initial concept had sparked a heated debate among the team. Some believed it was too ambitious, while others saw it as a game-changer. Laura listened intently, weighing the merits of each argument. After several rounds of discussion, she synthesized the divergent viewpoints into a strategic plan that addressed the concerns while retaining the innovative spirit of the original idea.

In the end, the product launch was a resounding success, far exceeding market expectations. The team's collective input had not only shaped a superior product but had also fostered a deep sense of ownership and pride among the employees. Laura's leadership style had transformed the company into a dynamic, agile, and resilient organization capable of navigating the complexities of the tech industry.

Laura's approach was a testament to the power of democratic leadership in the corporate world. By creating an environment where every team member felt their voice mattered, she had unlocked a wellspring of creativity and commitment that drove the company to new heights. Her story became a case study in how CEOs could leverage the collective intelligence of their teams to make informed, innovative decisions.

LAISSEZ-FAIRE LEADERSHIP

In the heart of Silicon Valley, where innovation and creativity thrive, there was a CEO named Jonathan who led his company, TechNova, with an unconventional approach. Unlike the authoritative leaders who meticulously outlined every step for their teams, Jonathan opted for a different route, one that many found perplexing yet profoundly liberating. He believed in the power of autonomy, trusting his employees to navigate their own paths and make decisions independently.

Jonathan's leadership style was a breath of fresh air in a world where micromanagement often stifled innovation. He rarely interfered with his team's daily operations and instead provided them with the freedom to explore and experiment. His philosophy was simple: hire the best people, give them the resources they need, and step back. This hands-off approach, known as laissez-faire leadership, was not without its risks, but Jonathan was convinced that the potential rewards far outweighed them.

At TechNova, the office buzzed with energy. Teams huddled together, brainstorming new ideas, and developers worked late into the night, driven by passion rather than obligation. Jonathan's trust in his employees fostered a culture of ownership and accountability. When challenges arose, the team didn't look to him for answers; they took it upon themselves to find solutions. This sense of responsibility empowered them and ignited a spirit of innovation that permeated the entire organization.

One might wonder how a company could thrive without a strong guiding hand. The answer lay in the meticulous selection of talent and the establishment of a clear vision. Jonathan was discerning in his hiring process, seeking individuals who not only possessed exceptional skills but also shared his vision for the future. He believed that with the right people in place, the company could achieve greatness without the need for constant oversight.

Jonathan's approach was not without its skeptics. Some board members and industry peers questioned the efficacy of such a leadership style, fearing it could lead to chaos and disorganization. However, the results spoke for themselves. Under Jonathan's leadership, TechNova experienced unprecedented growth, launching groundbreaking products that disrupted the market and garnered widespread acclaim.

One notable instance of the success of Jonathan's leadership style was the development of the company's flagship product, the NovaX. The idea for the NovaX came from a group of young engineers who, inspired by their freedom to innovate, conceptualized a revolutionary piece of technology. They pitched the idea to Jonathan, who gave them his full support and the autonomy to bring their vision to life. The project flourished, and the NovaX became one of TechNova's most successful products, catapulting the company to new heights.

Jonathan's laissez-faire leadership created an environment where creativity could flourish. It wasn't about abandoning responsibility but about empowering others to take the lead. He provided strategic direction and set the overall goals, but he trusted his team to determine the best way to achieve them. This trust was a powerful motivator, driving employees to exceed expectations and push the boundaries of what was possible.

In the fast-paced and ever-evolving tech industry, Jonathan's leadership style proved to be a game-changer. His belief in the capabilities of his team and his willingness to relinquish control allowed TechNova to become a beacon of innovation. Through his hands-off approach, Jonathan demonstrated that sometimes, the best way to lead is to let go.

TRANSFORMATIONAL LEADERSHIP

As the sun began to cast long shadows across the sleek boardroom, the atmosphere was charged with anticipation. The team had gathered, each individual bringing their unique expertise and perspectives, ready to tackle the challenge that lay ahead. The CEO, a figure of quiet confidence and vision, stood at the head of the table, ready to guide them through another critical decision-making process.

He was not just a leader by title but a beacon of inspiration for his team. His leadership style was neither authoritarian nor laissez-faire; it was something more dynamic, more engaging. He had the uncanny ability to see beyond the immediate, to envision a future that others might only glimpse in their dreams. This was not about incremental improvements or minor adjustments; it was about transformation, about turning the ordinary into the extraordinary.

He began the meeting not with directives but with questions. "What do we want to achieve?" he asked, his eyes scanning the room, inviting each person to contribute their thoughts. This was his way—engaging everyone, making them feel that their voices mattered. It was not just a strategy; it was a philosophy. He believed that leadership was not about holding power but about empowering others.

The discussion flowed freely, ideas bouncing off the walls like sparks in a forge. The CEO listened intently, his mind weaving the diverse threads into a coherent tapestry. He had a gift for identifying the potential in each suggestion, recognizing the seeds of greatness that others might overlook. His questions were probing yet respectful, challenging his team to think deeper, to push their boundaries.

He often shared stories of other leaders who had dared to dream big, who had transformed their organizations by fostering a culture of innovation and trust. These narratives were not just anecdotes; they were lessons, blueprints for what was possible. He spoke of leaders who had turned failing companies into industry giants, who had inspired their teams to achieve what seemed impossible. These stories were his way of showing that transformation was not a distant ideal but a tangible goal.

The CEO also knew the importance of personal growth. He encouraged his team to pursue their own development, to seek out new experiences and knowledge. He believed that a leader's strength lay in their ability to grow and adapt, to be a perpetual student of life. This commitment to personal and professional growth was infectious, creating a culture where everyone felt motivated to strive for excellence.

Trust was the cornerstone of his leadership. He trusted his team to make decisions, to take risks, to learn from their mistakes. This trust was not given lightly; it was earned through mutual respect and shared values. He understood that true transformation required a foundation of trust, where people felt safe to express their ideas and take bold steps.

As the meeting drew to a close, the CEO summarized the key points, weaving them into a vision that was both ambitious and attainable. He did not dictate the path forward; instead, he illuminated it, guiding his team with a steady hand and an open heart. They left the room not just with a plan but with a renewed sense of purpose, ready to turn vision into reality.

In the end, it was not just about achieving business goals; it was about transforming lives, about creating a legacy of innovation, trust, and growth. The CEO knew that true leadership was not about being in charge but about taking care of those in your charge, about inspiring them to reach heights they never thought possible. And in doing so, he was not just leading a company; he was transforming it.

CHAPTER EIGHT

Overcoming Decision-Making Challenges

COMMON PITFALLS

The sun had barely risen over the bustling cityscape when Laura, the newly-appointed CEO of a burgeoning tech startup, found herself staring at her reflection in the mirror. The responsibility of steering a ship in the uncharted waters of corporate leadership weighed heavily on her shoulders. As she mulled over the decisions she had to make, Laura knew that the path ahead was fraught with potential missteps. She had read countless books and articles, but nothing could fully prepare her for the labyrinthine maze of executive decision-making.

Laura's first board meeting was a daunting affair. Everyone seemed to have an opinion, and the pressure to make swift, impactful decisions was palpable. She remembered the advice of her predecessor, a seasoned veteran who had always emphasized the importance of data-driven decisions. Yet, in her eagerness to prove herself, Laura found herself swayed by the most vocal opinions in the room. She approved a risky project based on the enthusiasm of a charismatic team member, disregarding the lack of substantial data to support the venture. It wasn't long before the project floundered, and Laura was left to pick up the pieces.

It dawned on her that relying on gut feelings and persuasive voices was a common pitfall for many CEOs. The allure of a quick win often overshadowed the necessity for thorough analysis and due diligence. Laura realized that she needed to cultivate a balanced approach, one that combined intuition with empirical evidence.

As weeks turned into months, Laura faced another challenge: the temptation to micromanage. She had always been a hands-on leader, but as a CEO, her role demanded a different kind of oversight. Her initial attempts to involve herself in every minor detail led to burnout and frustration among her team. The company's progress slowed, and innovation was stifled. It was a hard lesson, but Laura learned that effective delegation was crucial. Trusting her team and empowering them to make decisions not only lightened her load but also fostered a culture of accountability and creativity.

Laura also found herself grappling with the fear of failure. The weight of expectations, both internal and external, created a paralyzing effect. She hesitated to make bold decisions, opting instead for safe, conservative choices that offered limited growth potential. It took a candid conversation with a mentor to help her understand that failure was an inevitable part of the journey. Embracing calculated risks was essential for innovation and long-term success.

Another revelation came when Laura noticed the tendency to stick with familiar strategies and resist change. The comfort of the known often led to complacency, and Laura saw how this mindset could stifle growth. She made a conscious effort to foster a culture of continuous improvement, encouraging her team to challenge the status quo and explore new avenues.

Navigating the intricate web of corporate leadership, Laura encountered numerous obstacles that tested her resolve. Each misstep offered valuable lessons, shaping her into a more resilient and insightful leader. She understood that the path to effective decision-making was not a linear one, but a journey of constant learning and adaptation. Through her experiences, Laura discovered that the key to successful leadership lay in recognizing and overcoming these common pitfalls, transforming challenges into opportunities for growth.

DEALING WITH UNCERTAINTY

In the high-stakes world of executive decision-making, the landscape is often shrouded in fog. CEOs are frequently required to make crucial choices without having all the pieces of the puzzle. The ability to navigate this uncertainty is what sets exceptional leaders apart from the rest.

Consider the tale of Laura Bennett, the CEO of a burgeoning tech startup. Laura found herself at a crossroads when her company faced a sudden market shift. Competitors were launching innovative products, and her team was scrambling to keep up. The data was incomplete, the stakes were high, and the clock was ticking. It was a scenario that would test any leader's mettle.

Laura's first step was to acknowledge the gaps in her information. Instead of being paralyzed by what she didn't know, she focused on what she did know. She gathered her key team members and facilitated a brainstorming session, encouraging them to share their insights and hypotheses. This collaborative approach allowed her to piece together a more comprehensive picture of the situation.

Next, Laura tapped into her network of industry experts and mentors. She reached out to seasoned professionals who had navigated similar storms. Their experiences provided valuable perspectives and helped her to weigh the potential risks and rewards of different strategies. Through these conversations, Laura gained a clearer understanding of the possible scenarios and their implications.

With a more informed viewpoint, Laura turned to scenario planning. She and her team mapped out various potential outcomes based on the available data and expert insights. They assessed the likelihood and impact of each scenario, allowing them to prioritize their actions and allocate resources more effectively. This exercise not only prepared them for different eventualities but also fostered a sense of readiness and confidence within the team.

Laura also recognized the importance of staying agile. She implemented a decision-making framework that allowed for flexibility and rapid response. By setting up regular check-ins and feedback loops, she ensured that her team could quickly pivot as new information emerged. This adaptive approach minimized the paralysis that often accompanies uncertainty and kept the company moving forward.

Throughout this process, Laura maintained transparent communication with her stakeholders. She openly shared the challenges and the rationale behind her decisions, building trust and buy-in from her team and investors. This transparency was crucial in aligning everyone's efforts towards a common goal, even when the path was not entirely clear.

In the end, Laura's ability to deal with uncertainty was not about having a foolproof plan, but about being prepared to adapt and respond to the unknown. She leveraged her resources, stayed flexible, and maintained clear communication, all while keeping her team focused and motivated. Her story underscores the essence of effective decision-making in uncertain times: it's about making the best possible choices with the information at hand and being ready to adjust as new information comes to light.

The journey of a CEO is seldom straightforward. The ability to navigate through the fog of uncertainty, to make decisions with conviction amidst ambiguity, defines the strength and resilience of a leader. Laura Bennett's experience is a testament to the power of informed agility and collaborative foresight in steering a company through uncharted waters.

MANAGING STRESS

The boardroom was buzzing with energy as the quarterly results were about to be unveiled. Alex, the CEO of a rapidly growing tech company, could feel the weight of the world pressing down on his shoulders. He had been here before, countless times, but the stress never seemed to get any easier to manage. The stakes were always high, and the pressure to perform was unrelenting.

Alex recalled a conversation he had with Sarah, a fellow CEO and close confidant. Over coffee, they often shared their struggles and triumphs, finding solace in the understanding that they weren't alone in their battles. Sarah had once told him, "Stress is like a shadow; it follows you wherever you go. The trick is not to outrun it, but to learn how to walk with it."

These words resonated deeply with Alex. He realized that acknowledging stress was the first step in managing it. Denial only compounded the problem, leading to burnout and poor decision-making. By recognizing the presence of stress, he could take proactive measures to mitigate its impact.

One of the techniques Alex employed was mindfulness. He had discovered the power of being present in the moment through his wife, who practiced yoga. Initially skeptical, he tried it reluctantly. Over time, he found that taking just a few minutes each day to focus on his breathing and clear his mind made a significant difference. It wasn't about emptying his thoughts but rather about observing them without judgment, allowing him to gain clarity and perspective.

Exercise became another crucial aspect of Alex's stress management strategy. He wasn't a natural athlete, but he committed to a routine that included running and weightlifting. The physical exertion not only improved his health but also served as a mental release. The rhythmic pounding of his feet on the pavement became a form of meditation, helping him to process his thoughts and emotions.

Alex also understood the importance of delegation. Early in his career, he had fallen into the trap of micromanaging, believing that he needed to control every aspect of the business to ensure success. This approach was unsustainable and led to unnecessary stress. By building a capable and trustworthy team, he learned to delegate responsibilities, freeing up his time to focus on strategic decisions. This shift not only reduced his stress but also empowered his team, fostering a culture of collaboration and innovation.

Another lesson Alex learned was the value of setting boundaries. The demands of being a CEO were endless, and it was easy to let work consume every waking moment. He made a conscious effort to carve out time for his family and personal interests. Whether it was attending his daughter's soccer games or enjoying a quiet dinner with his wife, these moments provided a much-needed respite from the rigors of his professional life.

Support networks played a pivotal role in Alex's ability to manage stress. He surrounded himself with mentors, peers, and friends who offered guidance, encouragement, and a listening ear. These relationships were a lifeline, providing him with different perspectives and reminding him that he wasn't alone in his journey.

As the quarterly results were announced, Alex felt a familiar surge of anxiety. But this time, he was prepared. He took a deep breath, grounded himself in the present, and reminded himself of the strategies he had put in place. Stress was a constant companion, but it no longer dictated his actions. Instead, it became a catalyst for growth, pushing him to become a more resilient and effective leader.

LEARNING FROM MISTAKES

The boardroom was silent, a tense atmosphere hanging in the air like a storm cloud. Mark, the CEO of a rapidly growing tech company, had just shared the news of a major setback. The ambitious product launch, which had consumed countless hours and resources, was a flop. Sales were dismal, and the market response was tepid at best. The disappointment was palpable, but Mark knew this moment was crucial.

Mark stood at the head of the table, his gaze steady. He took a deep breath and broke the silence. "We need to dissect what went wrong," he began, "not to assign blame, but to understand and learn." His voice carried a tone of resolve, echoing the principles that had guided him throughout his career.

He recalled a similar situation early in his tenure as a CEO. Back then, the failure of a key project had rattled him to his core. The memory of sleepless nights and endless self-doubt was still vivid. But it was during this challenging period that he discovered a fundamental truth: mistakes are not the end, but a beginning. They are lessons wrapped in adversity, offering insights that success often conceals.

Mark encouraged his team to speak openly. One by one, they began to analyze the decisions made, the assumptions held, and the signals missed. The marketing director acknowledged that the target audience had been misjudged. The product manager admitted that critical feedback during the beta phase had been overlooked. The finance officer pointed out that budget allocations had been overly optimistic.

As the discussion unfolded, Mark noticed a shift in the room. The initial defensiveness gave way to a collective determination to understand and improve. He shared his own insights, emphasizing that every misstep had the potential to refine their strategies and sharpen their instincts.

He recounted a story from his earlier days, when he had launched a software product that was ahead of its time. The market wasn't ready, and the venture failed spectacularly. It was a humbling experience, but it taught him to balance innovation with market readiness. That lesson had since become a cornerstone of his decision-making process.

Mark's approach wasn't just about identifying what went wrong, but also about recognizing what went right. He highlighted the team's dedication, the innovative features that had potential, and the valuable data gathered from the launch. These elements, he stressed, were the building blocks for future success.

The meeting concluded with a renewed sense of purpose. The team left the boardroom not with a sense of defeat, but with a roadmap for improvement. Mark knew that the real value of this experience lay in their ability to apply these lessons to future endeavors.

In the weeks that followed, the company implemented changes based on their findings. Market research became more rigorous, feedback loops were tightened, and resource allocation was approached with greater caution. The results were evident in their next project, which saw a much more favorable reception.

Mark's philosophy of learning from mistakes became ingrained in the company culture. It fostered an environment where risks were taken thoughtfully, and failures were viewed as opportunities for growth. This mindset not only strengthened their decision-making but also built resilience within the team.

Mark often reflected on that pivotal meeting. It wasn't the failure itself that defined their journey, but how they responded to it. Each mistake had been a stepping stone, guiding them toward better decisions and ultimately, greater success.

CHAPTER NINE

Building a Decision-Making Framework

ESTABLISHING CRITERIA

In the high-stakes world of corporate leadership, decisions can shape the direction of entire industries. For CEOs, the process of making these decisions is both an art and a science. It's a delicate balance of intuition, experience, and data-driven analysis. At the heart of this complex process lies the establishment of criteria—a foundational step that, though often overlooked, is crucial for making informed and effective decisions.

Imagine stepping into the shoes of a CEO, where every choice carries the weight of potential success or failure for the company. The first task is to clarify what success looks like. Without clear criteria, decisions can become muddled and directionless. This clarity begins with understanding the overarching goals of the organization. Are you aiming for rapid growth, market expansion, or perhaps innovation in product development? Each goal requires a different set of criteria to guide decision-making.

Consider the example of a CEO of a tech startup. The company is at a crossroads, deciding whether to pivot its product focus or double down on its current strategy. The criteria for this decision might include market potential, alignment with core competencies, and resource availability. By defining these criteria, the CEO can evaluate options through a lens that aligns with the company's strategic objectives.

But criteria are not just about aligning with goals; they also serve to mitigate risks. A seasoned CEO knows that every decision carries inherent risks, and establishing criteria helps to identify and weigh these risks effectively. For instance, when contemplating a merger or acquisition, criteria such as cultural fit, financial stability, and potential synergies become paramount. These criteria act as a safeguard, ensuring that decisions are not just beneficial but sustainable in the long term.

Moreover, criteria must be adaptable. The business landscape is ever-changing, and rigid criteria can become obsolete quickly. This requires a CEO to be both vigilant and flexible, constantly reassessing and adjusting criteria as new information and circumstances arise. Take the example of a retail CEO navigating the shift to e-commerce. Initially, criteria might focus on online market presence and digital infrastructure. However, as the transition progresses, criteria may need to evolve to include customer experience and data analytics capabilities.

In practice, establishing criteria is a collaborative process. While the final decision rests with the CEO, input from key stakeholders is invaluable. This includes insights from senior management, feedback from employees, and even perspectives from customers and partners. By incorporating diverse viewpoints, a CEO can establish more comprehensive and robust criteria, leading to better-informed decisions.

The role of data cannot be overstated in this process. In today's data-driven world, CEOs have access to an unprecedented amount of information. Leveraging this data to establish criteria ensures that decisions are grounded in reality rather than assumptions. For example, a CEO deciding on a new market entry might use data on consumer behavior, competitive landscape, and economic indicators to set criteria that accurately reflect market conditions.

Ultimately, the establishment of criteria is not a one-time task but an ongoing discipline. It requires a CEO to be introspective, analytical, and forward-thinking. By carefully defining and continuously refining criteria, CEOs can navigate the complexities of their role with greater confidence and clarity, leading their organizations toward sustained success.

INVOLVING STAKEHOLDERS

Margaret sat at the head of the long mahogany table, her fingers drumming lightly on the polished surface. The room, filled with the company's top executives, buzzed with subdued conversations. She glanced at her watch and cleared her throat, signaling the start of the meeting. All eyes turned towards her, the expectant silence magnifying the weight of her next words.

"Thank you all for being here," she began, her voice steady and commanding. "Today, we need to discuss our new strategic initiative and, more importantly, how we bring our stakeholders into the fold."

As Margaret spoke, she reflected on the lessons she'd learned over her years as CEO. Decisions made in isolation often led to unforeseen pitfalls. The most successful initiatives were those where stakeholders felt a sense of ownership and alignment with the company's vision. She knew that involving them from the outset was not just a tactic; it was a necessity.

Across the table, Jonathan, the CFO, adjusted his glasses and nodded. He had seen firsthand the financial repercussions of ignoring stakeholder input. Revenue projections had been missed, and projects had floundered simply because they failed to resonate with the very people they were designed to benefit.

Margaret continued, "Our stakeholders are not just investors or board members. They include our employees, customers, suppliers, and even the communities we operate in. Each group has its unique perspective and vested interest in our success. We must ensure their voices are heard."

She recalled a time early in her career when a major product launch had nearly derailed. The product, though innovative, had failed to gain traction in the market. It was only after they consulted their customer base that they realized the issue. The product had been designed without considering the end-user's needs. That costly mistake had taught her the invaluable lesson of stakeholder engagement.

David, the head of marketing, leaned forward. "We should begin with a comprehensive stakeholder analysis. Identify who our key stakeholders are, understand their concerns, and anticipate their needs. This will guide our communication strategy and help us build stronger relationships."

Margaret agreed, emphasizing the importance of transparency. "Open communication is critical. We need to be clear about our goals, the challenges we face, and the steps we're taking to address them. This builds trust and fosters a collaborative environment."

As the discussion progressed, ideas flowed freely around the table. The head of HR suggested regular town hall meetings to keep employees informed and engaged. The supplier relations manager proposed quarterly reviews with key suppliers to ensure alignment and address any concerns promptly. The community outreach director recommended creating a feedback loop with local communities to ensure their needs were met and to build goodwill.

Margaret felt a sense of optimism as she listened to her team. She knew that by involving stakeholders, they were not only making better decisions but also building a foundation of trust and mutual respect. This approach would lead to more sustainable and successful outcomes for the company.

As the meeting drew to a close, she looked around the room, seeing the determination in her team's eyes. They were ready to move forward, united in their commitment to involving stakeholders at every step. Margaret felt confident that this collaborative approach would guide them through the complexities of the business landscape, ensuring that their decisions were well-informed and widely supported.

IMPLEMENTING DECISIONS

When the decision has been made, the real challenge begins. CEOs often find themselves at a crossroads, where the clarity of their vision must be translated into concrete actions. This is the juncture where leadership is truly tested, and the ability to navigate complexities becomes paramount.

For Maria, the CEO of a mid-sized tech firm, the decision to pivot towards artificial intelligence was a monumental one. Her board had agreed, the strategy was clear, and the resources were allocated. Yet, as she sat in her office late one night, she realized the enormity of the task ahead. Implementing this decision required more than just a plan; it demanded meticulous execution and unwavering commitment.

Maria knew that communication was key. She called an all-hands meeting, where she laid out the vision with passion and clarity. Her team needed to understand not just the what, but the why and the how. She emphasized the importance of this pivot, painting a vivid picture of the future they were all working towards. The room buzzed with excitement, but Maria was acutely aware that enthusiasm alone wouldn't suffice.

She formed cross-functional teams, each tasked with specific objectives aligned with the broader strategy. Engineers, marketers, and product managers found themselves working side by side, breaking down silos that had long hindered collaboration. Maria appointed team leaders who were not just skilled, but also deeply committed to the vision. These leaders became her lieutenants, charged with driving the initiative forward.

Tracking progress became an obsession. Maria instituted weekly check-ins and quarterly reviews, where teams presented their achievements and setbacks. These sessions were not mere formalities; they were critical touchpoints for recalibrating efforts and ensuring alignment. Maria encouraged a culture of transparency, where challenges were openly discussed and solutions collaboratively crafted.

Resistance was inevitable. Some employees, comfortable in their existing roles, struggled to adapt to the new direction. Maria anticipated this and invested in training programs to upskill her workforce. She also created forums for open dialogue, where concerns could be voiced and addressed. Slowly, the skeptics began to see the value in the change, their apprehensions giving way to cautious optimism.

Resource allocation required surgical precision. Maria and her finance team scrutinized budgets, reallocating funds from less critical projects to the AI initiative. This was a delicate balancing act, as she needed to ensure that other essential operations continued to run smoothly. Each dollar spent was tracked, each investment evaluated for its return. The financial discipline was rigorous, yet Maria remained flexible, ready to pivot as new data emerged.

Maria understood the importance of celebrating milestones. Small victories were acknowledged, and major achievements were celebrated with gusto. These moments of recognition fueled morale, reinforcing the sense of collective purpose. The journey was arduous, but each success, no matter how small, was a testament to their collective effort.

Months turned into a year, and the fruits of their labor began to show. The company's AI-driven products started gaining traction in the market, attracting new customers and boosting revenue. Maria reflected on the path they had taken, recognizing that the success was not just in the decision itself, but in the relentless execution. The vision had been clear, but it was the meticulous planning, unwavering commitment, and the collective effort of her team that had turned it into reality.

Maria's experience underscored a fundamental truth for CEOs: making a decision is merely the first step. It is in the implementation where true leadership shines, where visions are transformed into tangible outcomes. The journey from decision to execution is fraught with challenges, but it is also where the most profound growth and success are found.

EVALUATING OUTCOMES

In the labyrinth of executive decision-making, the aftermath of choices reveals the true mettle of a CEO. Decisions are not mere actions taken in a vacuum; they ripple through the organization, touching every facet of the company. The most effective CEOs understand that evaluating the outcomes of their decisions is a critical step in refining their leadership.

The process of evaluating outcomes begins with setting clear, measurable objectives at the outset. Without defined goals, gauging success becomes an exercise in futility. These objectives act as a compass, guiding the organization and providing a benchmark against which outcomes can be assessed. When a CEO establishes these metrics, it not only clarifies expectations but also galvanizes the team towards a unified vision.

Once a decision is executed, the next phase is to gather data. This isn't just about numbers on a spreadsheet; it's about understanding the qualitative impact as well. Employee morale, customer satisfaction, and market perception are equally vital indicators. A CEO must cultivate a culture where feedback flows freely, creating an environment where insights from every level of the organization are valued. This holistic approach ensures a comprehensive understanding of the decision's impact.

The analysis of this data requires a blend of analytical rigor and intuitive understanding. CEOs must sift through the quantitative metrics, discerning patterns and trends, while also tuning into the subtler, qualitative feedback. This dual approach allows for a nuanced evaluation, recognizing that not all outcomes can be captured through sheer numbers.

One critical aspect of this evaluation is timing. Immediate results can be misleading, as some decisions yield their true impact only over time. A premature assessment might overlook long-term benefits or costs. Therefore, a CEO must strike a balance, periodically revisiting the decision's impact to capture its full spectrum. This iterative process demands patience and persistence, qualities that distinguish effective leaders.

Transparency plays a crucial role in this phase. Sharing the outcomes, both positive and negative, with the organization fosters a culture of accountability and continuous improvement. When a CEO openly communicates the results, it builds trust and reinforces the importance of learning from every decision. This transparency also encourages a growth mindset within the team, where failures are viewed as opportunities for learning rather than setbacks.

The final step in evaluating outcomes is reflection and adjustment. Armed with insights from the evaluation, a CEO must be willing to pivot, recalibrate, and refine strategies. This adaptability is the hallmark of resilient leadership. It involves a candid acknowledgment of what worked, what didn't, and what can be improved. This reflective process not only enhances future decision-making but also cultivates an organizational culture that values agility and innovation.

In the ever-evolving landscape of business, the ability to critically evaluate the outcomes of decisions is indispensable. It transforms leadership from a series of isolated choices into a continuous, dynamic process of learning and growth. For a CEO, this means not just steering the company towards immediate goals but also charting a course for sustained success.

CHAPTER TEN

Case Studies of Successful CEOs

TECH INDUSTRY LEADERS

In the gleaming offices of Silicon Valley, where innovation is the lifeblood and disruption the norm, decisions are made that shape the future of the world. The CEOs of these tech behemoths are not just leaders; they are visionaries, often making decisions that appear enigmatic to the uninitiated. To understand how these leaders decide, one must delve into their psyche, their environment, and the unique pressures they face.

Take, for instance, the story of Alex, the CEO of a leading artificial intelligence company. Alex's day begins before dawn, with a solitary run through the quiet streets of Palo Alto. This is not just a fitness routine; it's a mental exercise. As his feet pound the pavement, Alex contemplates the complex web of choices awaiting him. The solitude of the early morning hours provides an unbroken stream of thought, allowing him to sift through the myriad of data points, forecasts, and potential outcomes that will inform his decisions.

In the high-stakes world of tech, decisions are rarely straightforward. Alex must weigh the promise of groundbreaking innovation against the ethical implications of unleashing powerful AI systems into the world. His team, a diverse group of engineers, ethicists, and business strategists, provides a mosaic of perspectives. They gather in a glass-walled conference room, a symbol of the transparency and openness that Alex champions.

Here, discussions are intense, often bordering on the philosophical. The team debates the potential societal impacts of their technology, the competitive landscape, and the regulatory environment. Alex listens intently, not just to the words, but to the undercurrents of passion and concern that drive his team. He knows that the best decisions are rarely made in isolation. They are forged in the crucible of diverse viewpoints and rigorous debate.

Yet, there is another layer to Alex's decision-making process, one that is deeply personal. As a child of immigrant parents, he carries the weight of their sacrifices and the hopes they pinned on his success. This heritage instills in him a profound sense of responsibility. Each decision he makes is not just about the company's bottom line but about contributing to a legacy of progress and opportunity.

Across the valley, another CEO, Maria, leads a pioneering biotech firm. Her decisions are guided by a different set of principles. Maria's background as a scientist means she approaches problems with a meticulous, evidence-based mindset. Her lab coat may have been replaced by a tailored suit, but her commitment to data and empirical evidence remains unwavering.

Maria's decision-making process involves extensive consultations with her team of researchers and medical experts. She demands data, peer-reviewed studies, and clinical trial results before making any strategic move. But Maria also possesses an intuitive sense for the potential of her company's innovations. She understands that in biotech, the stakes are incredibly high, with the potential to save lives or alter the course of human health.

For both Alex and Maria, the role of a CEO in the tech industry is a delicate balance of vision and pragmatism. They must navigate a landscape where the pace of change is relentless, and the consequences of their decisions reverberate far beyond their companies. Their ability to decide effectively is not just a matter of intellect, but of character, intuition, and an unwavering commitment to their broader mission.

FINANCE INDUSTRY LEADERS

In the high-stakes world of finance, decisions are the lifeblood that keep the industry pulsating. The CEOs at the helm of major financial institutions wield unparalleled influence, steering their organizations through turbulent markets, regulatory changes, and economic upheavals. Their decision-making processes are a blend of meticulous analysis, intuition, and sheer audacity.

Take, for instance, the legendary Warren Buffett, CEO of Berkshire Hathaway, whose investment decisions have become the gold standard in the industry. Buffett's approach is rooted in value investing, a philosophy he inherited from his mentor, Benjamin Graham. His decisions are characterized by a deep understanding of intrinsic value, rigorous analysis of financial statements, and an almost unparalleled patience. He famously avoids following market trends, instead opting for what he calls "economic moats"—businesses with durable competitive advantages. His acquisition of companies like Geico and BNSF Railway were not just transactions; they were calculated moves based on decades of industry knowledge and a vision for long-term growth.

On the other side of the Atlantic, Ana Botín, Executive Chairman of Banco Santander, exemplifies a different, yet equally compelling, decision-making style. Botín's tenure has been marked by a focus on innovation and digital transformation. She has navigated the complexities of European banking regulations while also expanding Santander's footprint in Latin America. Her decisions often reflect a balance between technological advancement and traditional banking values. For Botín, the future of finance lies in leveraging technology to enhance customer experience and operational efficiency. Her strategic choices, from acquiring fintech startups to implementing AI-driven customer service platforms, highlight a forward-thinking mindset that is reshaping the banking landscape.

Jamie Dimon, CEO of JPMorgan Chase, is another luminary whose decision-making acumen has earned widespread acclaim. Dimon's leadership during the 2008 financial crisis is often cited as a masterclass in crisis management. His ability to make swift, decisive actions—such as the acquisition of Bear Stearns and Washington Mutual—helped stabilize not just his own institution but also contributed to broader market stability. Dimon's approach is a blend of pragmatism and innovation. He is known for his hands-on management style, often diving deep into the minutiae of operations. His decisions are informed by a comprehensive understanding of both macroeconomic trends and granular financial data, making him one of the most respected figures in the industry.

Abigail Johnson, CEO of Fidelity Investments, offers yet another perspective on decision-making in finance. As the leader of one of the world's largest asset management firms, Johnson has overseen a period of significant growth and transformation. Her decisions are often guided by a commitment to customer-centric innovation. Under her leadership, Fidelity has embraced digital tools and platforms, providing investors with more accessible and user-friendly ways to manage their portfolios. Johnson's focus on integrating technology with financial services reflects a broader industry trend, but her execution sets her apart. Her decisions are characterized by a blend of strategic foresight and a deep understanding of customer needs.

These leaders, with their diverse approaches, highlight the multifaceted nature of decision-making in the finance industry. Their choices are not merely reactions to external pressures but are often proactive strategies designed to position their organizations for long-term success. Through their actions, they demonstrate that effective decision-making in finance is as much about understanding the past and present as it is about envisioning the future.

HEALTHCARE INDUSTRY LEADERS

In the bustling corridors of the healthcare sector, decisions are not merely choices but lifelines. Each decision can ripple through the lives of millions, influencing patient outcomes, medical advancements, and the very fabric of society. This high-stakes environment demands a unique breed of leaders. These leaders must combine clinical knowledge with business acumen, empathy with efficiency, and innovation with ethics.

Take Dr. Samantha Greene, CEO of a leading healthcare network. Her journey from a practicing physician to a top executive was not a straight path but a labyrinth of complex decisions. Early in her career, she faced a pivotal moment when she had to decide between continuing her promising career as a cardiologist or stepping into an administrative role. The decision was not easy. She loved the direct impact she had on her patients' lives, yet she was increasingly drawn to the idea of influencing healthcare on a larger scale. After much deliberation, she chose to transition into healthcare administration, a decision that would shape the future of her organization.

Dr. Greene's approach to decision-making is a blend of data-driven analysis and human-centric thinking. She often describes her method as a "diagnostic approach" to leadership. Just as a doctor would diagnose a patient by considering symptoms, medical history, and diagnostic tests, she evaluates business challenges by examining data, understanding the organizational history, and listening to her team. This holistic approach has led to groundbreaking initiatives in patient care and operational efficiency.

Across the country, another healthcare leader, James Liu, CEO of a biotech firm, faces a different set of challenges. His company focuses on developing cutting-edge treatments for rare diseases. The stakes are incredibly high, as each decision can mean the difference between life and death for patients with limited options. Liu's decision-making process is deeply rooted in scientific rigor. He leverages vast amounts of research data, collaborates with top scientists, and consults with ethicists to ensure that every decision aligns with the company's mission and ethical standards.

Liu recounts a particularly challenging decision when his company was on the brink of a breakthrough in gene therapy. The preliminary data was promising, but there were significant risks involved. The potential to save lives was immense, but so were the ethical implications of proceeding without fully understanding the long-term effects. Liu convened a diverse panel of experts, including scientists, ethicists, and patient advocates, to deliberate on the best course of action. This inclusive approach ensured that the decision was not only scientifically sound but also ethically responsible.

In a different corner of the healthcare world, Maria Sanchez, CEO of a major pharmaceutical company, navigates a landscape fraught with regulatory hurdles and public scrutiny. Her decision-making process is a masterclass in balancing innovation with compliance.

One of her most notable decisions involved the development of a new vaccine. The pressure was immense, with public health crises looming and the world watching. Sanchez prioritized transparency and collaboration, working closely with regulatory bodies, healthcare providers, and the public. This open approach not only expedited the approval process but also built public trust.

These leaders, with their diverse backgrounds and unique challenges, exemplify the multifaceted nature of decision-making in the healthcare industry. Their stories illuminate how the best decisions are often a delicate balance of data, ethics, and human insight. Whether they are steering a hospital, a biotech firm, or a pharmaceutical giant, their decisions resonate far beyond the boardroom, touching the lives of countless individuals and shaping the future of healthcare.

RETAIL INDUSTRY LEADERS

In the bustling world of retail, the CEOs who lead the charge are faced with a complex landscape of shifting consumer preferences, technological advancements, and fierce competition. The decisions they make not only shape their own companies but often set trends for the entire industry. These retail industry leaders are adept at reading the pulse of the market, anticipating changes, and steering their organizations through both calm and turbulent waters.

One such leader is Sarah Thompson, the CEO of a major retail chain that has become synonymous with innovation. When she took the helm, the company was struggling to keep up with the rapid pace of e-commerce growth. Traditional brick-and-mortar stores were losing foot traffic, and the online presence was lackluster. Sarah's first significant decision was to invest heavily in digital transformation. She understood that merely having an online store was not enough; the customer experience had to be seamless and engaging.

Under her leadership, the company rolled out a state-of-the-art mobile app, revamped its website, and integrated advanced analytics to personalize shopping experiences. Sarah's strategic vision extended beyond technology. She also recognized the importance of sustainability and ethical practices. By committing to eco-friendly products and transparent supply chains, she not only attracted a new demographic of environmentally-conscious consumers but also positioned the company as a responsible industry leader.

Another prominent figure is James Rodriguez, the CEO of a global fashion retailer. James faced a different set of challenges. The fashion industry is notoriously fickle, with trends changing almost overnight. To stay ahead, James had to foster a culture of agility and creativity within his organization. He encouraged his teams to take risks and experiment with bold ideas, whether it was through collaborations with avant-garde designers or the use of cutting-edge materials.

James's approach to decision-making is deeply collaborative. He believes that the best ideas often come from unexpected places within the company. By creating an open environment where employees at all levels can contribute, he has tapped into a wellspring of innovation that keeps the brand fresh and relevant. His emphasis on inclusivity and diversity has also resonated with a global audience, broadening the company's appeal and reach.

In contrast, consider the approach of Linda Chen, who leads a luxury retail brand known for its timeless elegance. Linda's decisions are guided by a deep respect for the brand's heritage and the craftsmanship that defines its products. She is meticulous in maintaining the quality and exclusivity that loyal customers expect. However, Linda is not averse to change. Recognizing the growing importance of digital channels, she has carefully integrated e-commerce into the brand's strategy without diluting its premium image.

Linda's leadership style is characterized by a balance between tradition and innovation. She has introduced limited-edition collections available exclusively online, creating a sense of urgency and exclusivity. This move has successfully bridged the gap between the brand's storied past and the modern consumer's expectations.

These retail industry leaders share a common thread: the ability to make strategic decisions that both respond to immediate challenges and lay the groundwork for future success. Whether through digital transformation, fostering creativity, or balancing tradition with innovation, their decisions are shaping the retail landscape in profound ways. Their stories offer valuable insights into the art and science of decision-making at the highest levels of business.

CHAPTER ELEVEN

THE GLOBAL PERSPECTIVE

CULTURAL INFLUENCES ON DECISION-MAKING

In the heart of Tokyo, a CEO sits in a minimalist office, gazing at the meticulously organized cityscape. Across the globe, in Silicon Valley, another CEO paces in a cluttered room filled with whiteboards and gadgets, brainstorming with a team. Despite their geographical and cultural differences, both are making decisions that will shape their companies' futures. The environments, values, and cultural norms surrounding them play a pivotal role in how these leaders approach decision-making.

In Japan, the concept of "nemawashi" is deeply ingrained in the business culture. This term, which literally means "going around the roots," refers to the informal process of laying the groundwork for a decision by talking to all stakeholders and gaining their support before any official meeting. For the Tokyo-based CEO, this means spending considerable time in one-on-one discussions, ensuring that everyone is on board before proceeding. This method may seem slow to an outsider, but in Japanese culture, it fosters consensus and harmony, which are valued above swift, unilateral decisions.

Meanwhile, in Silicon Valley, the ethos of "fail fast, fail often" dominates the entrepreneurial landscape. Here, the CEO is encouraged to make quick decisions, pivot when necessary, and embrace failure as a learning opportunity. The fast-paced, innovative environment rewards boldness and risk-taking. The decision-making process is more individualistic, often relying on the intuition and vision of the leader rather than a collective agreement. This approach can lead to rapid advancements and breakthroughs, but it also carries the risk of missteps and failures.

In contrast, a CEO in Germany might approach decision-making with a focus on precision and thoroughness. German business culture values detailed analysis, careful planning, and reliability. Decisions are often made after extensive research and consultation with experts. The process is methodical, with a strong emphasis on avoiding errors and ensuring long-term success. This meticulous approach can result in high-quality outcomes, but it may also slow down the decision-making process, making it less adaptable to rapidly changing environments.

In India, the business environment is characterized by its complexity and diversity. A CEO here must navigate a myriad of social, economic, and political factors. Decision-making often involves balancing traditional values with modern business practices. Relationships and personal connections play a significant role, and there is a high tolerance for ambiguity and flexibility. This adaptability allows Indian leaders to maneuver through uncertain and volatile situations, but it can also lead to inconsistency and unpredictability.

These examples illustrate how cultural contexts shape the way CEOs make decisions. Each approach has its strengths and weaknesses, and what works in one culture may not be effective in another. Understanding these cultural influences is crucial for any leader operating in a globalized world. It requires not only awareness but also the ability to adapt and integrate different decision-making styles.

As globalization continues to blur the boundaries between cultures, CEOs must become adept at navigating these diverse landscapes. They need to recognize the cultural underpinnings of their decision-making processes and those of their international counterparts. By doing so, they can foster better communication, collaboration, and ultimately, more effective decision-making across borders. The ability to bridge cultural differences and leverage the strengths of various decision-making styles can be a powerful asset in the complex, interconnected world of modern business.

GLOBAL ECONOMIC FACTORS

As the sun cast long shadows over the boardroom, the CEO of a multinational corporation sat at the head of the table, his fingers steepled in contemplation. The day's agenda was heavy, laden with decisions that could pivot the company's future. The conversation had shifted from internal metrics to the broader canvas of the global economy, a topic that demanded not only keen insight but also a nuanced understanding of interconnected markets.

The room was filled with the hum of anticipation. Each executive around the table knew that the decisions made today would be influenced by forces far beyond their control. The CEO broke the silence, his voice steady but tinged with the gravity of the situation. "We must consider the economic climate," he began. "From trade policies to currency fluctuations, our strategies must be agile enough to respond to external pressures."

Eyes turned to the Chief Economist, who had been meticulously tracking global trends. She highlighted the ongoing trade tensions between major economies. Tariffs and sanctions were not just abstract numbers; they translated into real costs for the company. The CEO nodded, recognizing that supply chain disruptions could ripple through their operations, affecting everything from raw material procurement to final product delivery.

Another layer of complexity was added by the fluctuating currencies. The CFO presented a detailed report, illustrating how the volatility of the dollar against emerging market currencies could erode profit margins. The CEO leaned back, absorbing the information. Hedging strategies were discussed, but they were not foolproof. The global economy was a living organism, unpredictable and ever-changing.

The conversation then pivoted to interest rates. The central banks' policies in different parts of the world were like puppeteers, pulling strings that affected borrowing costs and investment flows. The CEO's mind raced through the implications. Lower interest rates could spur investment but also indicated potential economic slowdowns. The balancing act was delicate, and the stakes were high.

Geopolitical risks were another critical factor. The CEO recalled a recent scenario planning session where various geopolitical developments were mapped out. Political instability in a key market could lead to abrupt regulatory changes, impacting operations and market access. The CEO knew that having contingency plans was essential, but predicting the exact nature and timing of such risks was akin to reading tea leaves.

The discussion was rounded out by considering technological disruptions. The global economy was not static, and technological advancements were reshaping industries at a breathtaking pace. The CEO pondered the dual nature of technology as both an opportunity and a threat. Embracing innovation could lead to competitive advantages, but it also required significant investment and carried the risk of obsolescence.

As the meeting drew to a close, the CEO summarized the multifaceted nature of the global economic landscape. It was clear that making informed decisions required a holistic view, one that integrated various economic indicators and trends. The external environment was a mosaic of challenges and opportunities, and navigating it demanded both strategic foresight and operational flexibility.

The CEO rose from his chair, the weight of the global economy resting on his shoulders. He glanced around the room, meeting the eyes of his team. Each executive understood the gravity of their roles. The decisions made in this room would not only shape the company's trajectory but also ripple through the markets they served. The global economic factors were not mere background noise; they were the symphony to which every decision must harmonize.

INTERNATIONAL CASE STUDIES

In the bustling metropolis of Tokyo, Hiroshi Tanaka faced a critical decision that would shape the future of his multinational corporation. The company, renowned for its innovative electronics, was at a crossroads. With competitors closing in and market demands evolving rapidly, Tanaka knew that a bold move was necessary. He convened his top executives in a sleek, glass-walled conference room overlooking the cityscape. The atmosphere was charged with anticipation as Tanaka presented his vision: a strategic partnership with a leading AI firm based in Silicon Valley. The team deliberated, weighing the potential risks and rewards. After hours of intense discussion, they reached a consensus. The partnership was announced, and within months, the company unveiled a groundbreaking product that set a new industry standard.

Across the Atlantic, in the heart of Berlin, Maria Schneider, the CEO of a sustainable fashion brand, grappled with a different kind of challenge. Her company had built a loyal customer base by championing eco-friendly practices. However, a recent scandal involving one of their suppliers threatened to tarnish their reputation. Schneider knew that transparency and swift action were imperative. She organized a press conference, where she addressed the issue head-on, detailing the steps the company would take to rectify the situation and ensure it never happened again. Her candid approach not only restored customer trust but also reinforced the brand's commitment to sustainability.

Meanwhile, in São Paulo, Carlos Mendes, the head of a rapidly growing fintech startup, was navigating the complexities of scaling his business. The Brazilian market was ripe with opportunities, but also fraught with regulatory hurdles. Mendes had to decide whether to expand domestically or venture into the broader Latin American market. He gathered insights from his advisory board, conducted extensive market research, and even sought the counsel of his competitors. After a thorough analysis, Mendes opted for a phased expansion, starting with neighboring countries that had similar regulatory frameworks. This calculated approach allowed the company to grow steadily while mitigating potential risks.

In Johannesburg, Amina Nkosi, the CEO of a pioneering healthcare technology firm, was on the brink of a major breakthrough. Her team had developed a cutting-edge telemedicine platform designed to improve access to healthcare in remote areas. The challenge was securing funding to scale the project. Nkosi embarked on a series of high-stakes meetings with potential investors, each one more demanding than the last. Her unwavering passion and clear vision for the future of healthcare eventually won over a prominent venture capital firm. The investment not only propelled the platform to new heights but also revolutionized healthcare delivery in underserved communities.

Each of these CEOs, operating in vastly different contexts, showcased a unique approach to decision-making. Tanaka's strategic foresight, Schneider's integrity, Mendes's analytical rigor, and Nkosi's tenacity exemplified the diverse qualities that define effective leadership. Their stories, though distinct, shared a common thread: the ability to navigate uncertainty with confidence and conviction. These international case studies illustrate that while the challenges may vary, the principles of decisive leadership remain universally applicable.

ADAPTING TO GLOBAL MARKETS

The CEO of a burgeoning tech company sat in his sleek, glass-walled office, overlooking the bustling city below. His mind was a whirlwind of thoughts as he reviewed the latest reports from the international markets. It was clear that their domestic success had reached a plateau, and the next logical step was to expand globally. Yet, the complexities of international markets were daunting.

He remembered a conversation with a mentor who had once led a successful expansion into Asia. "It's not just about translating your product's language," the mentor had said. "You need to understand the culture, the local business practices, and even the subtle nuances of consumer behavior." These words echoed in his mind as he pondered the next move.

The CEO initiated a series of meetings with his leadership team. Each session was a deep dive into the intricacies of potential markets. They scrutinized economic indicators, regulatory environments, and competitive landscapes. The marketing director brought in data showing how consumer preferences varied dramatically across regions. What appealed to customers in Europe might not resonate with those in South America or Asia.

One critical decision was to hire local experts. The CEO believed that no amount of market research could replace the insights of someone who lived and breathed the local culture. They brought on board a seasoned executive from Brazil, who had a keen understanding of the Latin American market. Her insights were invaluable, revealing that their product needed significant adaptation to meet local tastes and expectations.

The team also explored partnerships with local firms. This strategy provided a dual advantage: it offered an immediate understanding of the market and a built-in distribution network. They partnered with a well-established company in India, which not only smoothed the entry into the market but also lent credibility to their brand.

The CEO knew that entering a new market required more than just a strategic plan. It demanded flexibility and a willingness to iterate. They launched pilot projects in select cities, using these as test beds to refine their approach. These pilots were closely monitored, with rapid feedback loops allowing for swift adjustments. The initial results were mixed, but the team remained undeterred, learning from each setback and celebrating small victories.

One of the most significant challenges was navigating the regulatory landscape. Each country had its own set of rules, and non-compliance could lead to costly delays or even legal troubles. The CEO brought in a team of legal experts specializing in international business law. Their task was to ensure that every aspect of their operation, from product standards to marketing practices, adhered to local regulations.

The cultural adaptation went beyond the product itself. The company's branding and messaging had to resonate with local values and traditions. They discovered that in some markets, a hard-sell approach was off-putting, while in others, it was expected. The marketing team crafted tailored campaigns, each reflecting the unique ethos of the target market.

The CEO also recognized the importance of internal alignment. Expanding globally was not just an external endeavor; it required a shift in the company's mindset. He initiated training programs to equip employees with the skills and cultural sensitivity needed for international operations. This internal transformation was crucial, ensuring that the entire organization was prepared for the challenges and opportunities of global markets.

As the months passed, the company began to see the fruits of its labor. Sales in new markets started to pick up, and the brand gained recognition beyond its home country. The CEO knew that this was just the beginning. The global market was vast and ever-changing, but with a solid foundation and a nimble approach, they were well-positioned to navigate its complexities.

CHAPTER TWELVE

Technological Impact on Decisions

ROLE OF AI AND MACHINE LEARNING

In the dimly lit boardroom, the CEO leaned back in his chair, fingers steepled, eyes fixed on the array of numbers projected on the screen. It was a critical moment, one that would shape the company's future. Yet, unlike in the past, he wasn't relying solely on his gut instinct or the insights of his trusted advisors. He had a new ally—one that could process vast amounts of data in the blink of an eye and uncover patterns invisible to the human eye.

Artificial Intelligence and Machine Learning were no longer the stuff of science fiction. They had become indispensable tools in the decision-making arsenal of modern CEOs. The CEO in the boardroom understood this well. He had seen firsthand how these technologies could transform raw data into actionable insights, enabling him to make informed decisions with unprecedented speed and accuracy.

AI and Machine Learning algorithms could sift through mountains of data, identifying trends and anomalies that would take human analysts weeks, if not months, to uncover. They could predict market shifts, customer preferences, and even potential risks, providing a level of foresight that was once unimaginable. For the CEO, this meant staying ahead of the competition, anticipating changes, and adapting strategies with agility.

But the power of AI and Machine Learning extended beyond mere data analysis. These technologies could simulate various scenarios, allowing the CEO to explore the potential outcomes of different decisions. By running simulations, he could assess the impact of each choice on the company's bottom line, weigh the risks and benefits, and choose the path that offered the greatest potential for success.

The CEO also appreciated that AI and Machine Learning could enhance collaboration within the organization. By breaking down silos and integrating data from different departments, these technologies fostered a more holistic view of the business. Marketing, finance, operations, and HR could all contribute their insights, creating a richer, more comprehensive picture of the company's performance and prospects.

Moreover, AI and Machine Learning could automate routine tasks, freeing up valuable time for the CEO and his team to focus on strategic initiatives. The monotonous chore of data entry, the tedious process of generating reports, the repetitive task of monitoring KPIs—all of these could be handled by intelligent systems, allowing human minds to concentrate on higher-order thinking and innovation.

Yet, the CEO was acutely aware of the limitations and ethical considerations that came with these powerful tools. He knew that algorithms were only as good as the data they were trained on, and that biased or incomplete data could lead to flawed conclusions. He was also mindful of the potential for AI to displace human workers, and he was committed to using these technologies responsibly, ensuring that they complemented rather than replaced the human element.

As the meeting progressed, the CEO made his decisions with confidence, backed by the insights provided by AI and Machine Learning. He felt a sense of empowerment, knowing that he was leveraging the full potential of these technologies to drive the company forward. The future was uncertain, but with AI and Machine Learning by his side, he was better equipped to navigate the complexities of the business world and steer his company toward success.

DIGITAL TRANSFORMATION

Amidst the clamor of quarterly earnings calls and the incessant hum of boardroom discussions, a new force began to permeate the air: the whisper of digital transformation. CEOs found themselves at a crossroads, where traditional business models met the relentless advance of technology. The decision to pivot wasn't merely about adopting new tools; it was about reshaping entire organizations to thrive in an era defined by rapid technological change.

In the heart of this transformation lay the realization that data had become the new currency. Leaders who once relied on intuition and experience were now turning to analytics and algorithms. The ability to harness vast amounts of information and distill it into actionable insights granted a competitive edge that was impossible to ignore. Companies that invested in data infrastructure found themselves better positioned to anticipate market shifts, understand customer behavior, and optimize operations.

Yet, the journey was far from straightforward. For many CEOs, the initial steps involved a deep dive into unfamiliar waters. Legacy systems, often the backbone of their enterprises, presented both a challenge and an opportunity. Modernizing these systems required a delicate balance: retaining the reliability of established processes while infusing them with the agility and innovation of new technologies. This often meant significant investments in IT, along with a cultural shift towards a more tech-savvy workforce.

The human element of digital transformation proved to be as critical as the technological one. Employees needed to be brought along on this journey, their skills and mindsets evolving in tandem with the tools they were given. Training programs, workshops, and a culture of continuous learning became pivotal. CEOs who successfully navigated this terrain did so by fostering an environment where experimentation was encouraged, and failure was seen as a stepping stone rather than a setback.

Customer expectations, too, were evolving at a breakneck pace. The digital age had empowered consumers with unprecedented access to information and choices. Meeting their demands required a level of personalization and responsiveness that traditional methods could not match. Businesses began leveraging artificial intelligence and machine learning to deliver tailored experiences, predict needs, and engage with customers in real time. The ability to offer seamless, omnichannel experiences became a hallmark of successful digital transformation.

Moreover, the very definition of competition was undergoing a metamorphosis. Start-ups, unburdened by legacy constraints and often more nimble, posed significant threats to established players. In response, some CEOs chose to forge alliances with these disruptors, investing in or acquiring innovative companies to bolster their own capabilities. Others opted for internal innovation labs, fostering a start-up mentality within their own walls.

Regulatory landscapes, too, were shifting, with governments around the world grappling to keep pace with technological advancements. Navigating these changes required a keen understanding of both local and global regulatory requirements, ensuring compliance while pushing the boundaries of innovation.

The stories of those who succeeded in digital transformation were often marked by a willingness to take calculated risks, to pivot when necessary, and to stay resilient in the face of setbacks. It was a journey that required not just a change in tools and processes, but a fundamental shift in mindset—a recognition that in the digital age, the only constant is change itself.

In this new era, the role of the CEO had evolved. No longer just a steward of the present, they had become architects of the future, guiding their organizations through the uncharted territories of digital transformation, armed with vision, courage, and an unwavering commitment to innovation.

CYBERSECURITY CONSIDERATIONS

As dawn breaks over the sprawling cityscape, CEOs everywhere are already deep in thought, contemplating the myriad decisions that will shape the future of their enterprises. Among these, one decision stands out starkly against the backdrop of our hyper-connected world: the safeguarding of digital assets. Cybersecurity is no longer a mere technical issue relegated to IT departments; it is a critical strategic concern that commands the full attention of the C-suite.

In the boardroom, the discussion often starts with a simple yet profound question: What is at stake? For modern businesses, the answer is everything. Intellectual property, customer data, financial records, and even the operational continuity of the company hang in the balance. The digital transformation that has enabled unprecedented growth and innovation also exposes vulnerabilities that can be exploited by malicious actors. CEOs must navigate this complex terrain with both vigilance and foresight.

Consider the case of a multinational corporation that recently fell victim to a sophisticated cyberattack. The breach was not just a technical failure but a strategic disaster. Sensitive customer data was compromised, leading to a loss of trust and a significant financial hit. The CEO, once confident in the company's robust growth trajectory, found herself grappling with a crisis that threatened to undo years of hard work. This incident underscored the critical need for a proactive and comprehensive approach to cybersecurity.

The conversation soon turns to the role of leadership in fostering a culture of security. It is not enough to invest in the latest technologies; the human element is equally crucial. A CEO's commitment to cybersecurity must permeate every level of the organization. This means regular training for employees, clear communication of security policies, and an environment where vigilance is a shared responsibility. When every team member understands the importance of cybersecurity and their role in maintaining it, the organization becomes inherently more resilient.

Next, the focus shifts to the strategic alignment of cybersecurity with business objectives. CEOs must ensure that their cybersecurity strategy is not an isolated set of practices but integrated into the overall business strategy. This alignment involves understanding the specific threats that their industry faces and tailoring their defenses accordingly. For instance, a financial services firm might prioritize the protection of transactional data, while a healthcare provider focuses on safeguarding patient records.

Partnerships and collaboration also emerge as key themes. In an increasingly interconnected world, no organization is an island. CEOs recognize the value of working with external experts, industry peers, and even competitors to enhance their cybersecurity posture. Information sharing about threats and best practices can create a collective defense that is stronger than any single entity could achieve alone.

The narrative then delves into the emerging trends that CEOs must keep an eye on. The rise of artificial intelligence, the proliferation of Internet of Things devices, and the advent of quantum computing are all double-edged swords. While they offer tremendous opportunities for innovation, they also introduce new vulnerabilities. Forward-thinking CEOs must stay informed about these developments and be prepared to adapt their strategies accordingly.

Ultimately, the CEO's role in cybersecurity is multifaceted. It involves not only making informed decisions about technology and policy but also leading by example and fostering a culture of security. As the protector of the company's future, the CEO must be ever vigilant, ever proactive, and ever ready to respond to the evolving landscape of digital threats. The stakes are high, but with the right approach, the rewards of a secure and resilient organization are well within reach.

FUTURE TECHNOLOGICAL TRENDS

The room was filled with the hum of anticipation as the board members settled into their seats, their eyes fixed on the CEO standing at the head of the table. He looked around the room, a small smile playing at the corners of his mouth. "Let's talk about what's coming," he began, his voice steady but tinged with excitement. "The future isn't just an abstract concept for us; it's a series of decisions we need to make today."

The CEO tapped a button on his presentation remote, and the first slide illuminated the wall behind him. It was a graph showing the exponential growth of artificial intelligence capabilities over the past decade. "AI isn't just about automating tasks anymore. It's about augmenting human decision-making processes. Think of our customer service chatbots. They're not just answering questions; they're learning from each interaction, becoming more efficient, more human-like. Imagine applying that to our data analytics, our market predictions. The decisions we make could be backed by insights we can't even fathom right now."

He paused, letting the implications sink in. The next slide featured a sleek, modern factory. "Automation and robotics are transforming manufacturing. We're talking about precision and efficiency at levels we've never seen before. But it's not just about replacing human labor; it's about collaboration. Cobots—collaborative robots—are working side by side with humans, enhancing our capabilities rather than diminishing them. This isn't the future of work; it's the present, and it's evolving fast."

The CEO moved to the next point, his tone growing more passionate. "Blockchain technology isn't just for cryptocurrencies. Its potential for secure, transparent transactions can revolutionize supply chains, ensuring authenticity and traceability from start to finish. Imagine a world where every component of our products can be tracked in real-time, reducing fraud and increasing trust. This is more than a trend; it's a paradigm shift."

He clicked the remote again, and a new slide appeared, showcasing a virtual reality headset. "Immersive technologies like VR and AR are not just for gaming anymore. They're transforming training, design, and customer experience. Imagine virtual prototypes that can be manipulated in real-time, or training programs that simulate real-world scenarios without the risk. These technologies can offer us a competitive edge in ways we haven't yet explored fully."

The room was silent, the weight of the information settling over the board members. The CEO's eyes twinkled as he moved to the final slide, which displayed a network of interconnected devices. "The Internet of Things is creating a world where everything is connected. Smart sensors in our products can provide real-time data, allowing us to monitor performance, predict maintenance needs, and improve user experience. This interconnectedness isn't just about convenience; it's about creating a seamless, intelligent ecosystem."

He looked around the room, meeting each board member's gaze. "These technological trends aren't just about staying current; they're about staying ahead. The decisions we make today will define our place in the market tomorrow. We need to be proactive, not reactive. We need to invest in these technologies, understand their implications, and integrate them into our strategic planning."

The CEO's voice softened, but his message was clear. "The future is coming faster than we think. Our challenge is to not just keep up, but to lead. To make decisions that will not only benefit our company but shape the industry. This is our opportunity, and it's up to us to seize it."

CHAPTER THIRTEEN

Crisis Management

IDENTIFYING A CRISIS

A ringing phone broke the silence of the early morning. Clara Martinez, CEO of a thriving tech startup, glanced at the caller ID. It was her head of public relations, Lisa. Clara's instincts told her that this wasn't a routine call. She picked up, bracing herself for the unknown.

"Clara, we have a situation," Lisa's voice trembled slightly. The words hung in the air, heavy with implication. Clara's mind raced. A situation, in corporate speak, often meant a crisis. She quickly moved to her office, closing the door behind her.

Lisa continued, "There's been a data breach. It's all over social media. Customers are already reacting, and we're trending for all the wrong reasons."

Clara's heart sank. The company had invested millions in cybersecurity, but now wasn't the time for recriminations. She needed facts. "How bad is it?" she asked, her voice steady despite the storm brewing inside her.

"Preliminary reports suggest that personal information of at least 10,000 users has been compromised. We're still assessing the full extent," Lisa replied, her tone professional but laden with concern.

Clara's mind went into overdrive. Identifying a crisis is the first step in managing it, she recalled from a seminar she once attended. The words of the speaker echoed in her mind: "A crisis is a turning point. It's the moment when a situation either spirals out of control or gets contained."

She needed to gather her team immediately. Clara pressed a button on her intercom, summoning her chief technology officer, head of legal, and director of customer service. They arrived within minutes, their expressions mirroring her own anxiety.

"Here's where we stand," Clara briefed them. "We have a data breach affecting thousands of our users. We need to assess the damage, communicate transparently, and take immediate action to secure our systems."

The CTO, Mark, spoke first. "We're already working on identifying the breach point and sealing it. Our initial findings indicate it might be due to a vulnerability in third-party software we integrated last month."

"Legal implications?" Clara turned to Sarah, her head of legal.

"We need to notify affected users and regulatory authorities within 72 hours to comply with GDPR and other data protection laws. We should also prepare for potential lawsuits," Sarah responded, her voice calm but firm.

Clara nodded. "Customer service?"

Tom, the director of customer service, was already strategizing.

"We need to set up a dedicated hotline and an email response team. Transparency will be key. Users need to know we're on top of this."

As her team dispersed to tackle their respective tasks, Clara took a moment to breathe. The initial shock was wearing off, replaced by a steely resolve. Identifying the crisis was just the beginning. The real challenge lay in the decisions that followed.

She opened her laptop and began drafting a message to the company's employees. They needed to hear from her directly. Trust within the organization was as crucial as the trust of their users.

"Team," she typed, "we are facing a significant challenge. A data breach has compromised the personal information of many of our users. Our priority is to address this swiftly and transparently. I have full confidence in our ability to navigate this crisis together. Let's stay focused and support each other through this."

As she hit send, Clara felt a sense of clarity. The crisis was identified. Now it was time to lead.

RAPID DECISION-MAKING

In the high-stakes world of corporate leadership, decisions often need to be made swiftly and with conviction. The ability to make rapid decisions, without sacrificing quality, is a hallmark of successful CEOs. It's a skill honed through experience, intuition, and a refined understanding of the business landscape.

Consider the scenario: a sudden market shift threatens to disrupt the core operations of a company. The CEO is faced with a choice—pivot the strategy or stay the course. Time is of the essence. In such moments, hesitation can be costly. The CEO taps into a deep reservoir of knowledge and instinct, accumulated over years of navigating the volatile business environment. This is not a reckless gamble but a calculated risk, informed by data, insights from trusted advisors, and an acute awareness of the company's strengths and vulnerabilities.

Effective CEOs have a knack for filtering through noise and identifying the signal. They understand that not all information is created equal. In the age of information overload, discerning the relevant from the irrelevant is crucial. This ability to prioritize information allows them to make informed decisions quickly. They rely on a core team of advisors who provide concise, actionable insights, and they trust these advisors implicitly. Building such a team requires not only selecting individuals with the right expertise but also fostering a culture where candid communication is valued.

Speed in decision-making often involves a certain level of decisiveness and confidence. However, it is not about making decisions in isolation. The best CEOs create an environment where rapid decision-making is supported by robust processes and frameworks. They establish clear criteria for decision-making, ensuring that even under pressure, choices align with the company's strategic objectives and values. This approach minimizes the risk of impulsive decisions driven by short-term pressures.

A critical aspect of rapid decision-making is the willingness to iterate. CEOs recognize that not all decisions will be perfect from the outset. They are comfortable with the concept of course correction. This iterative process involves making a decision, assessing its impact, and making necessary adjustments. It's a dynamic approach that allows for flexibility and responsiveness in an ever-changing market.

Moreover, the personal qualities of a CEO play a significant role. Emotional intelligence, resilience, and adaptability are indispensable. These attributes enable a CEO to remain calm under pressure, maintain clarity of thought, and inspire confidence within the organization. When a leader exudes confidence and composure, it permeates through the company, fostering a culture of agility and responsiveness.

In some cases, rapid decision-making also involves leveraging technology. Advanced data analytics, artificial intelligence, and machine learning can provide real-time insights, aiding CEOs in making swift, informed decisions. Embracing these technological tools can significantly enhance the decision-making process, providing a competitive edge in the fast-paced business environment.

The art of rapid decision-making is a delicate balance between speed and precision. It requires a blend of intuition, experience, and strategic thinking. CEOs who master this art not only navigate their companies through turbulent times but also seize opportunities that others might miss. Their ability to make quick, yet sound decisions, propels their organizations forward, ensuring sustained growth and resilience in the face of uncertainty.

COMMUNICATION STRATEGIES

The boardroom was silent as the CEO, a seasoned leader with decades of experience, prepared to address his executive team. His eyes scanned the room, noting the anxious expressions of his colleagues. He knew that the success of their latest project hinged not just on strategy but on the way he communicated their next steps.

He began to speak, his tone calm and measured, each word chosen with precision. He knew that effective communication was the cornerstone of his leadership. He had learned early in his career that clarity and transparency were essential in guiding his team through complex decisions. His approach was always to share the vision first, painting a vivid picture of the future they were working towards. This method not only inspired his team but also provided a clear direction, eliminating ambiguity and aligning everyone's efforts.

As he outlined the plan, he made sure to address potential concerns. He had an intuitive understanding of his team's fears and doubts, and he tackled them head-on. By acknowledging these issues, he fostered an environment of trust and openness. His team knew that they could voice their concerns without fear of retribution, which encouraged a culture of honest and constructive dialogue.

He then opened the floor to questions. This was not just a formality; it was a crucial part of his communication strategy. He believed that every question, no matter how trivial it seemed, was an opportunity to reinforce the plan and ensure everyone was on the same page. His responses were thorough and thoughtful, demonstrating his deep understanding of the project and his commitment to his team's success.

Throughout the discussion, he made it a point to listen actively. He understood that communication was a two-way street. By listening to his team's input, he not only gathered valuable insights but also made his team feel valued and respected. This sense of inclusion was vital in building a cohesive and motivated team.

He also used stories and analogies to illustrate his points. He knew that abstract concepts could be difficult to grasp, but by relating them to familiar experiences, he made them more accessible. These stories were not just about the successes but also the failures. He shared lessons learned from past mistakes, demonstrating that failure was not something to be feared but a stepping stone to success. This candidness made him relatable and trustworthy, qualities that were indispensable in his role as a leader.

Non-verbal communication played a significant role as well. His body language was open and confident, his gestures deliberate and meaningful. He maintained eye contact, signaling his engagement and sincerity. He was aware that his demeanor set the tone for the entire meeting. By projecting calm and confidence, he instilled the same feelings in his team.

After the meeting, he made it a point to follow up individually with key team members. These one-on-one interactions allowed him to address any lingering doubts and provide additional support. It also gave him a chance to gather feedback on his communication methods, always seeking ways to improve.

In the end, his communication strategy was not just about conveying information but about building a shared understanding and commitment. It was about creating an environment where everyone felt heard and valued, where the team could thrive and achieve their goals together. This approach, refined over years of leadership, was a testament to the power of effective communication in driving success.

POST-CRISIS EVALUATION

The boardroom was hushed, the atmosphere thick with the weight of recent events. The CEO, a seasoned leader with a silver streak in his hair, stood at the head of the table. His eyes scanned the room, taking in the expectant faces of his team. They had weathered a storm together, one that had tested their resolve and ingenuity. Now, it was time to dissect their actions, to understand what had worked, what had faltered, and how they could emerge stronger.

The first to speak was the Chief Operating Officer, a meticulous strategist known for her analytical mind. She presented a detailed timeline of the crisis, outlining key decisions and their immediate impacts. Her voice was steady, but there was an undercurrent of urgency. She highlighted the moments when their contingency plans had proved invaluable, but she did not shy away from pointing out the lapses. "We need to refine our response protocols," she said, her tone resolute. "There were gaps in our communication channels that led to delays."

The Chief Financial Officer, a man with a knack for numbers and a calm demeanor, nodded in agreement. He had already run the figures, comparing projected losses with actual outcomes. His report was thorough, revealing both the financial strain and the unexpected areas where they had managed to save costs. "Our liquidity cushion was a lifesaver," he remarked. "But we underestimated the duration of the crisis. We need a more flexible financial strategy."

As the discussion progressed, it became clear that this was not merely an exercise in fault-finding. Each leader brought their perspective, their insights forming a mosaic of the crisis response. The Chief Technology Officer, a visionary with a passion for innovation, spoke about the accelerated digital transformation. "Our pivot to remote work was smoother than anticipated," she noted. "However, our cybersecurity measures were not robust enough to handle the increased load. We need to invest in stronger defenses."

The Human Resources Director, a compassionate advocate for the employees, shared her observations. She talked about the emotional toll on the workforce, the spike in stress-related issues, and the measures they had implemented to support their teams. "Our mental health initiatives were crucial," she said. "But we need to build a more resilient organizational culture to better support our people in times of crisis."

The CEO listened intently, absorbing each point. He had always believed in the power of collective wisdom, in the idea that the best decisions emerged from diverse viewpoints. He saw the value in this post-crisis evaluation, not as a critique but as a learning opportunity. He encouraged open dialogue, asking probing questions and challenging assumptions.

The room was filled with a sense of purpose, a determination to learn and adapt. The leaders were not just reviewing the past; they were laying the groundwork for the future. They discussed new protocols, enhanced training programs, and strategic investments. They debated the merits of different approaches, weighing risks and benefits with renewed clarity.

In the heart of this process was a commitment to continuous improvement. The CEO knew that the true test of leadership was not just in navigating a crisis but in learning from it. He saw the potential for growth, the chance to build a more agile, resilient organization. As the meeting drew to a close, there was a palpable sense of resolve. They had faced the crisis together, and now, they were ready to forge a stronger path forward.

CHAPTER FOURTEEN

DECISION-MAKING TOOLS AND TECHNIQUES

DECISION TREES

In the first light of dawn, the CEO sits in their office, the weight of the company's future pressing heavily on their shoulders. They face a labyrinth of choices, each path branching into myriad possibilities. This intricate web of decisions can paralyze even the most seasoned leader. Yet, within this complexity lies a tool as old as strategy itself, yet as modern as artificial intelligence: the decision tree.

Imagine standing at the base of a grand oak tree, its branches stretching out in all directions. Each branch represents a potential decision, each leaf a possible outcome. The process begins with a single, critical question, the root of the tree. From this root, the tree unfurls, each branch splitting into smaller and smaller branches, each fork representing a decision point.

For the CEO, the decision tree is more than just a diagram; it is a map through the wilderness of uncertainty. It begins with the identification of the problem or opportunity at hand. This is the tree's trunk, solid and unwavering, representing the core issue that needs resolution. From there, the branches grow.

The first split represents the primary options available. For example, if the CEO is deciding whether to launch a new product, the initial branches might represent the choice between launching, delaying, or canceling the project. Each of these branches then splits further, representing the potential outcomes and subsequent decisions that follow each initial choice.

At each junction, the CEO must weigh the potential outcomes, considering both the probabilities of success and the potential risks. This is where the decision tree's power truly shines. By visualizing each possible path, the CEO can see not just the immediate consequences of a decision, but the ripple effects that follow. This holistic view allows for a more informed choice, one that takes into account the full spectrum of possibilities.

Moreover, decision trees are not static. They grow and evolve as new information becomes available. A savvy CEO revisits their decision trees regularly, pruning branches that no longer serve and nurturing new growth where opportunities arise. This dynamic approach ensures that decisions remain relevant and grounded in the latest data.

In the digital age, decision trees have become even more powerful tools. Advanced algorithms and machine learning models can analyze vast amounts of data, providing insights that were previously unimaginable. These technological advancements allow for even more precise and nuanced decision trees, giving CEOs a competitive edge in an increasingly complex business landscape.

Yet, despite their sophistication, the essence of decision trees remains rooted in simplicity. At their core, they are about breaking down complex decisions into manageable parts, allowing leaders to see the forest for the trees. They provide a structured framework for navigating uncertainty, turning what could be an overwhelming process into a series of clear, actionable steps.

As the CEO looks at the decision tree laid out before them, they see more than just a series of branches and leaves. They see a path through the fog of uncertainty, a way to bring clarity to chaos. With each decision they make, they shape the future of their company, one branch at a time. The decision tree becomes a living testament to their leadership, a map of their journey through the intricate web of choices that define their tenure.

COST-BENEFIT ANALYSIS

In the high-stakes world of corporate decision-making, every choice a CEO makes reverberates through the entire organization, impacting employees, shareholders, and the market at large. It's a delicate balance, where the weight of potential gains must be meticulously measured against the risks and costs. This is where the art and science of cost-benefit analysis come into play, a crucial tool in the CEO's arsenal.

Imagine a CEO, Sarah, at the helm of a burgeoning tech company. She's faced with a pivotal decision: whether to invest in a cutting-edge, yet unproven technology. The allure of being a market leader and the potential for exponential growth is tantalizing. However, the financial outlay and the uncertainty of return loom large. It's not a decision to be taken lightly, and Sarah knows that a methodical approach is essential.

Sarah gathers her executive team and dives into the intricate process of cost-benefit analysis. They start by identifying all potential costs associated with the investment. This isn't just about the initial financial expenditure. They consider the cost of research and development, the time required to bring the technology to market, potential disruptions to existing projects, and the opportunity cost of not investing those resources elsewhere.

Equally important are the intangible costs. They ponder over the potential impact on employee morale if the project fails, the possible damage to the company's reputation, and the strain on current partnerships. By laying out these factors, Sarah and her team create a comprehensive picture of what the company stands to lose.

On the other side of the equation, they scrutinize the benefits. The potential revenue from being the first to market with this technology is substantial. There's also the competitive advantage, the ability to attract top talent intrigued by the innovative work, and the long-term growth prospects. The team projects various scenarios, from the most optimistic to the most conservative, to gauge the range of possible outcomes.

The process is not purely quantitative. Sarah knows that numbers alone can't capture the full breadth of implications. She considers qualitative factors, such as the alignment of this new technology with the company's long-term vision and values. They discuss the potential for this technology to open new markets or create synergies with existing products.

As they delve deeper, Sarah's team employs sensitivity analysis to understand how changes in key assumptions might affect the outcome. They run simulations, tweaking variables like market adoption rates and development timelines, to see how resilient their projections are under different conditions. This helps them to identify the critical factors that could make or break the project.

Throughout this process, Sarah maintains a clear-eyed perspective, ensuring that the enthusiasm for innovation doesn't cloud their judgment. She seeks input from external experts, balancing internal optimism with external caution. By the time the analysis is complete, Sarah has a well-rounded view of the potential risks and rewards.

The decision-making process culminates in a board meeting, where Sarah presents the findings. Armed with a thorough cost-benefit analysis, she articulates the rationale behind the recommendation, addressing potential concerns and highlighting the strategic fit. The board, confident in the rigor of the analysis, gives their approval.

The decision to proceed is not just a leap of faith but a calculated move, informed by a meticulous evaluation of costs and benefits. It exemplifies how effective CEOs blend analytical rigor with strategic foresight, ensuring that every decision is not just a gamble but a step towards sustained success.

THE DELPHI METHOD

In the high-rise boardrooms where decisions can make or break a company, CEOs often find themselves navigating a labyrinth of uncertainties. Amidst this complexity, one method has emerged as a beacon of collective intelligence: the Delphi Method. This technique, named after the ancient Greek oracle, offers a structured approach to harnessing the wisdom of experts, providing a path to clarity in the murky waters of strategic decision-making.

Picture a roundtable of seasoned professionals, each bringing a wealth of experience and insight. Unlike conventional meetings where voices can be drowned out by the loudest or most persuasive, the Delphi Method levels the playing field. Here, anonymity is the cornerstone, ensuring that ideas are judged on their merit rather than the stature of the speaker. This process begins with a carefully curated panel of experts, selected for their knowledge and relevance to the issue at hand. These experts are then asked to respond to a series of questionnaires, delving into the nuances of the problem.

The beauty of this method lies in its iterative nature. After the initial responses are collected, a facilitator synthesizes the information, identifying common themes and divergent opinions. This synthesis is then fed back to the panel, prompting a new round of reflection and response. Through successive rounds, the experts refine their views, often converging towards a consensus or uncovering new perspectives that had previously been overlooked. This iterative feedback loop not only enhances the quality of the insights but also allows for a deeper understanding of the complexities involved.

For CEOs, the Delphi Method offers several distinct advantages. It mitigates the influence of dominant personalities, fostering a more democratic exchange of ideas. This is particularly valuable in environments where hierarchical structures can stifle open dialogue. Additionally, the anonymity of the process encourages candor, enabling experts to share their true opinions without fear of repercussions. This can be especially crucial when dealing with sensitive or contentious issues.

Consider the case of a company facing a major technological shift. The CEO, aware of the potential risks and opportunities, turns to the Delphi Method to chart a course forward. By engaging a panel of experts from diverse fields—technology, market analysis, finance, and consumer behavior—the CEO gains a multifaceted view of the landscape. Through the iterative rounds of the Delphi process, the experts' insights evolve, revealing not just the probable impacts of the technological shift but also the strategic moves that could position the company advantageously.

The Delphi Method is not without its challenges. It requires careful selection of experts and a skilled facilitator to manage the process. Moreover, the time required for multiple rounds of feedback can be a constraint in fast-paced decision-making environments. However, for decisions that demand thorough analysis and the synthesis of diverse viewpoints, the benefits far outweigh these hurdles.

In the realm of corporate strategy, where uncertainty is the only constant, the Delphi Method stands out as a robust tool for CEOs. It transforms the cacophony of expert opinions into a coherent symphony of insights, guiding leaders towards informed and balanced decisions. Through this method, CEOs can navigate the complexities of their roles with a clearer vision, bolstered by the collective wisdom of their expert panels.

SIX THINKING HATS

In the bustling heart of the corporate jungle, CEOs often find themselves at crossroads, facing decisions that could shape the destiny of their organizations. It was during one such critical juncture that Sarah, the CEO of a burgeoning tech startup, found herself grappling with a complex dilemma. Her team had developed a revolutionary product, but the path to market was fraught with uncertainty. Traditional decision-making strategies seemed inadequate to navigate the multifaceted challenges ahead.

Sarah remembered a technique she had encountered during a leadership workshop, a method pioneered by Edward de Bono called "Six Thinking Hats." This approach promised to dissect decisions from multiple angles, providing a structured yet creative framework for problem-solving. Intrigued by its potential, she decided to introduce it to her executive team.

Gathering her top advisors in the sleek, glass-walled conference room, Sarah explained the concept. "We will each wear different 'hats' to explore our decision from various perspectives," she began, sensing the curiosity in the room. "By doing so, we can uncover insights that might otherwise remain hidden."

First, they donned the White Hat, focusing on objective data and facts. Mark, the CFO, presented detailed market research, highlighting potential demand and competitive landscape. The team absorbed the information, recognizing the importance of grounding their decision in concrete evidence.

Next, the Red Hat allowed them to express their emotions and intuitions. Emily, the Chief Marketing Officer, voiced her excitement about the product's potential to disrupt the market. However, she also shared her anxiety about the significant investment required. This candid emotional exchange fostered empathy and understanding among the team members.

With the Black Hat, they examined potential risks and pitfalls. James, the Head of Operations, outlined logistical challenges and possible regulatory hurdles. His cautious perspective prompted the team to consider contingency plans, ensuring they were prepared for worst-case scenarios.

Switching to the Yellow Hat, they explored the optimistic view. Lisa, the Chief Innovation Officer, highlighted the product's unique features and the immense value it could bring to customers. Her enthusiasm was infectious, inspiring the team to envision the positive impact their innovation could achieve.

The Green Hat unleashed their creativity, encouraging them to brainstorm innovative solutions. Ideas flowed freely, from novel marketing strategies to unconventional distribution channels. This phase energized the team, revealing possibilities they hadn't previously considered.

Finally, with the Blue Hat, they took a step back to manage the thinking process. Sarah facilitated a discussion to synthesize their insights, ensuring that each perspective was integrated into their final decision. The structured approach provided clarity, helping them to see the bigger picture.

As the meeting concluded, Sarah felt a sense of accomplishment. The Six Thinking Hats had transformed what could have been a contentious debate into a collaborative exploration. The team had not only reached a well-rounded decision but also strengthened their collective resolve.

The product launch, guided by this multifaceted approach, turned out to be a resounding success. Sarah's decision to employ the Six Thinking Hats had proven invaluable, equipping her team with a holistic view that navigated them through uncertainty with confidence and creativity.

In the dynamic world of corporate leadership, where decisions often carry significant weight, the Six Thinking Hats provided a powerful tool for CEOs like Sarah. It reminded them that the best decisions come not from a single perspective but from the harmonious integration of diverse viewpoints.

CHAPTER FIFTEEN

Enhancing Personal Decision-Making Skills

SELF-REFLECTION

In the quiet moments before dawn, when the world is still and the mind finds a rare respite from the ceaseless demands of leadership, a CEO sits alone in contemplation. This is not mere meditation, but an essential practice that shapes the trajectory of their decisions. In those precious minutes, they traverse the vast landscape of their thoughts, examining the intricate web of choices, actions, and consequences that define their role.

A CEO's day is a relentless cascade of meetings, emails, and decisions, each one demanding a swift yet calculated response. Yet, amidst this whirlwind, the most profound decisions often stem from those tranquil moments of self-reflection. It's a practice that requires discipline and courage, for it is in these moments that one confronts the raw, unvarnished truths of their leadership.

The process begins with a simple question: "What am I trying to achieve?" This inquiry is not about quarterly targets or market share, but about the deeper purpose that drives the organization. The CEO delves into their core values, the mission that ignited their passion, and the vision that guides their every move. They weigh their recent decisions against these fundamental principles, scrutinizing whether their actions align with the greater good they aspire to create.

In this reflective state, a CEO must navigate the delicate balance between confidence and humility. Confidence is necessary to lead with conviction, to inspire trust and motivate the team. However, unchecked confidence can morph into hubris, blinding one to critical feedback and alternative perspectives. Humility, on the other hand, fosters a culture of openness and continuous learning. It allows a CEO to acknowledge mistakes, seek advice, and adapt to changing circumstances.

The CEO revisits past decisions, not with the intent to dwell on failures, but to extract valuable lessons. They analyze what went right, what went wrong, and why. This introspection is a powerful tool for growth, transforming missteps into stepping stones for future success. By understanding the root causes of their errors, they fortify their decision-making framework, ensuring that each choice is informed by experience and wisdom.

Self-reflection also compels a CEO to confront their biases and assumptions. Every leader carries with them a set of preconceived notions, shaped by their background, experiences, and worldview. These biases can cloud judgment and skew decisions. Through deliberate introspection, a CEO identifies these biases, challenges them, and actively seeks diverse perspectives to counterbalance their own.

Moreover, self-reflection fosters emotional intelligence, an indispensable trait for effective leadership. By tuning into their own emotions and understanding their impact, a CEO can better manage stress, communicate with empathy, and build stronger relationships within the organization. This emotional awareness extends to recognizing the emotional states of others, enabling the CEO to lead with compassion and forge a cohesive, resilient team.

In the grand tapestry of leadership, self-reflection is the thread that weaves clarity, integrity, and purpose into every decision. It is a solitary practice, yet its ripple effects resonate throughout the organization, shaping its culture and driving its success. As the first light of day breaks through the darkness, the CEO rises, their mind sharpened and their resolve strengthened. They are ready to face the challenges ahead, guided by the insights gleaned from their quiet introspection.

CONTINUOUS LEARNING

As the sun began its slow descent, casting a golden hue over the bustling cityscape, Elena Martinez pondered the path that had brought her to the helm of a multinational corporation. The role of a CEO was not just about making decisions; it was about making the right decisions, ones that could steer the company towards success or failure. She recalled the early days of her career, when she was fresh out of business school, armed with theories and strategies but lacking the wisdom that only experience could bring.

Elena's father, a seasoned entrepreneur himself, had often emphasized the importance of continuous learning. "The world never stops evolving," he would say, "and neither should you." At first, she had dismissed his advice as the nostalgic ramblings of an old man. But as she climbed the corporate ladder, she began to see the merit in his words. The business landscape was indeed ever-changing, with new technologies, market trends, and consumer behaviors constantly emerging. The key to staying ahead was not just to adapt but to anticipate these changes.

One evening, after a particularly challenging board meeting, Elena found herself reflecting on the concept of continuous learning. She realized that her most significant breakthroughs had come not from her formal education but from her willingness to learn from every situation, every setback, and every success. She remembered a pivotal moment early in her tenure as CEO when a major project had failed spectacularly. Instead of placing blame, she had gathered her team and dissected every aspect of the project to understand what went wrong. It was a humbling experience, but it taught her valuable lessons about risk management, team dynamics, and the importance of clear communication.

Elena also understood that continuous learning wasn't confined to the walls of the office. She made it a point to read extensively, not just business books but literature from various fields. She attended conferences, networked with other industry leaders, and even took online courses to keep her skills sharp. One of her favorite activities was engaging in deep, meaningful conversations with her employees, from the top executives to the entry-level staff. She believed that everyone had something to teach her, and these interactions often provided fresh perspectives and innovative ideas.

Mentorship played a crucial role in her learning journey as well. Elena sought out mentors who challenged her thinking and pushed her out of her comfort zone. She also became a mentor herself, finding that teaching others reinforced her own knowledge and skills. The reciprocal nature of mentorship created a dynamic learning environment where both parties grew together.

Elena's approach to continuous learning extended to her leadership style. She fostered a culture of curiosity within her company, encouraging her employees to pursue their own learning paths. She implemented programs that supported professional development, from workshops and seminars to tuition reimbursement for further education. This not only enhanced the skills of her workforce but also instilled a sense of loyalty and motivation.

As the last rays of sunlight disappeared behind the skyscrapers, Elena felt a deep sense of fulfillment. She knew that the journey of learning was never-ending, and that was what made it exciting. Each day brought new opportunities to grow, to innovate, and to make better decisions. And in the relentless pursuit of knowledge, she found the true essence of leadership.

SEEKING FEEDBACK

As the CEO of a burgeoning tech startup, Jonathan had always prided himself on his decisiveness. His company, InnovateX, had skyrocketed from a modest garage operation to a bustling enterprise with hundreds of employees. Jonathan's instincts had served him well, guiding the company through turbulent markets and competitive landscapes. Yet, as the stakes grew higher, he began to sense a subtle shift—an awareness that his intuition alone might not be enough to sustain their growth.

One crisp autumn morning, Jonathan found himself in his corner office, gazing out at the cityscape. The weight of a critical decision loomed over him: a potential merger with a promising AI company. The numbers made sense, and the strategic benefits were clear. Still, something gnawed at him, an internal voice urging caution. He realized he needed more than just his own perspective.

Jonathan decided to call a meeting with his executive team. As they gathered around the sleek conference table, he could see the curiosity in their eyes. He laid out the proposal, detailing the potential merger and its implications. The room buzzed with energy as his team began to dissect the information, offering insights from their unique vantage points.

Maria, the CFO, raised concerns about the financial risks involved. Her analytical mind had always complemented Jonathan's visionary approach, and her meticulous breakdown of the numbers revealed potential pitfalls he hadn't fully considered. Next, Raj, the Head of Product Development, highlighted the technological synergies that could propel their innovation forward. His excitement was palpable, and his enthusiasm began to sway some of the skeptics in the room.

Then, there was Emily, the Chief Marketing Officer, who brought a different angle to the discussion. She spoke about the brand implications and how the merger could reshape their market positioning. Her perspective was invaluable, shedding light on aspects that Jonathan had overlooked.

As the conversation unfolded, Jonathan felt a sense of clarity emerging. The diverse viewpoints of his team were like pieces of a puzzle, each contributing to a more comprehensive understanding of the situation. He realized that seeking feedback wasn't a sign of weakness but a strategic move to harness the collective wisdom of his leadership team.

Later that day, Jonathan took a walk through the office, engaging with employees from various departments. He initiated casual conversations, asking for their thoughts on the potential merger. The responses were varied, but each one offered a unique insight. A software engineer mentioned potential integration challenges, while a customer service representative highlighted concerns about client reactions.

These interactions reinforced Jonathan's belief in the power of feedback. He understood that his role as CEO wasn't just to make decisions but to create an environment where diverse perspectives could flourish. By actively seeking input from his team and employees, he was building a foundation of trust and collaboration.

That evening, Jonathan sat down with his thoughts. The feedback he had gathered painted a nuanced picture, helping him weigh the pros and cons more effectively. He felt a renewed sense of confidence, not just in the decision he was about to make, but in the process that had led him there.

Jonathan knew that the path ahead would be challenging, but he was no longer walking it alone. The collective intelligence of InnovateX was now his greatest asset, guiding him through the complexities of leadership and decision-making.

BUILDING CONFIDENCE

Under the dim glow of the conference room lights, James, a newly-appointed CEO, found himself grappling with a sense of inadequacy. The weight of decision-making pressed heavily on his shoulders. The board members, seasoned veterans of the corporate world, watched him closely, their expectations palpable. James knew that his first major decision would set the tone for his tenure and determine whether he would gain the trust of his team.

As the meeting wore on, his mind drifted to a conversation he had with his mentor, Eleanor, a retired CEO known for her decisiveness and unshakeable confidence. Eleanor had once told him, "Confidence isn’t about knowing everything; it’s about trusting yourself to handle whatever comes your way." Those words resonated deeply with James, but in the moment, they felt like a distant echo.

James decided to take a step back and focus on what he could control. He began by seeking out information, diving into reports, and understanding the intricacies of the situation at hand. He knew that knowledge was a powerful ally, but he also understood that overloading himself with data could be paralyzing. It was a delicate balance.

He reached out to his team, engaging in open dialogues and encouraging them to share their insights and concerns. By fostering an environment of trust and collaboration, James not only gathered valuable perspectives but also began to build a foundation of mutual respect. He realized that confidence could be cultivated through collective wisdom.

One evening, while poring over documents in his office, an idea struck him. He recalled Eleanor's practice of visualizing success. She would imagine the outcome she desired and work backward, identifying the steps needed to achieve it. James decided to give it a try. He closed his eyes and pictured the successful implementation of his decision, the positive impact it would have on the company, and the sense of accomplishment that would follow.

The visualization exercise provided James with a renewed sense of clarity and purpose. He started to see potential obstacles not as insurmountable challenges but as opportunities for growth and learning. This shift in perspective was pivotal. It allowed him to approach the decision with a mindset of resilience and adaptability.

With his newfound confidence, James presented his plan to the board. He spoke with conviction, outlining the rationale behind his decision and the benefits it would bring. He acknowledged the risks but emphasized the strategic measures in place to mitigate them. His demeanor exuded assurance, and the board members responded positively, their initial skepticism giving way to support.

James's journey to building confidence was not a solitary one. It was shaped by the guidance of mentors, the collaboration of his team, and his own willingness to embrace uncertainty. He learned that confidence is not a static trait but a dynamic process, one that requires continuous effort and self-reflection.

As he left the conference room that day, James felt a sense of accomplishment. He understood that confidence was not about having all the answers but about having the courage to make decisions and the resilience to navigate the outcomes. It was about trusting himself and his team, and knowing that together, they could face any challenge that came their way.

CHAPTER SIXTEEN

LET'S CHECK YOUR DECISION MAKING SKILLS

QUESTIONNAIRE TO JUDGE YOUR DECISION MAKING SKILLS

Answer the following questions as honestly as possible. For each question, choose the option that best describes your typical behavior or preference. Your responses will be scored to categorize your decision-making personality.

Questionnaire:

1. When faced with a difficult decision, what is your usual approach?
   a) I analyze all available data and consider all possible outcomes.
   b) I rely on my intuition and gut feeling.
   c) I ask for advice from others and consider their opinions.
   d) I make a quick decision to avoid overthinking.

2. How do you handle unexpected changes or disruptions to your plans?
   a) I remain calm and quickly adapt to the new situation.
   b) I get stressed but eventually adjust.
   c) I seek input from others to find the best way forward.
   d) I struggle to cope and may become indecisive.

3. When making a significant purchase, such as a car or a house, what is your process?
   a) I research extensively and compare all options.
   b) I go with what feels right in the moment.
   c) I discuss with family or friends before deciding.
   d) I make a quick decision to avoid wasting time.

4. How do you prioritize tasks when you have multiple deadlines?
   a) I create a detailed plan and stick to it.
   b) I handle tasks as they come, based on urgency.
   c) I consult with others to decide what to tackle first.
   d) I often find it hard to prioritize and may end up procrastinating.

5. In a team setting, how do you contribute to decision-making?
   a) I analyze the pros and cons and present my findings.
   b) I suggest ideas based on my instincts.
   c) I encourage discussion and seek consensus.
   d) I prefer to let others take the lead in decision-making.

6. When you realize you've made a wrong decision, what is your reaction?
   a) I analyze what went wrong and learn from the mistake.
   b) I accept it as a part of life and move on quickly.
   c) I seek feedback to understand different perspectives.
   d) I feel regretful and may hesitate to make future decisions.

7. How do you approach learning new skills or information?
   a) I research thoroughly and practice consistently.
   b) I dive in and learn through experience.
   c) I learn best through collaborative efforts and group activities.
   d) I may start enthusiastically but often lose interest quickly.

8. What is your response to high-pressure situations?
   a) I stay calm, assess the situation, and act logically.
   b) I rely on my instincts to guide me.
   c) I look for support and guidance from others.
   d) I tend to get overwhelmed and may struggle to act.

9. How do you make decisions about your career path?
   a) I carefully evaluate all options and consider long-term implications.
   b) I follow my passions and interests, even if the path is uncertain.
   c) I seek advice from mentors and peers.
   d) I take opportunities as they come, without much planning.

10. When planning a vacation, what is your style?
   a) I meticulously plan every detail and make a schedule.
   b) I choose a destination and go with the flow.
   c) I ask friends and family for recommendations.
   d) I make last-minute decisions and go spontaneously.

11. How do you handle conflicts with colleagues or peers?
   a) I address the issue directly and logically.
   b) I follow my instincts to resolve the conflict.
   c) I involve a mediator or seek advice from others.
   d) I try to avoid confrontation and let it resolve on its own.

12. How do you choose which books or movies to read/watch?
    a) I research reviews and ratings extensively.
    b) I pick based on what catches my eye or intuition.
    c) I go with recommendations from friends or family.
    d) I make a quick choice without much thought.

13. What is your approach to investing money?
    a) I conduct thorough research and seek professional advice.
    b) I invest based on my intuition and market trends.
    c) I discuss options with financially savvy friends or family.
    d) I make quick decisions to capitalize on immediate opportunities.

4. When solving a complex problem, how do you start?
    a) I break it down into smaller, manageable parts.
    b) I brainstorm solutions and go with what feels right.
    c) I gather a team to discuss and find a solution together.
    d) I dive in and address issues as they come.

15. How do you handle feedback or criticism?
    a) I analyze it objectively and use it to improve.
    b) I trust my gut on whether to accept or ignore it.
    c) I discuss it with others to get their perspectives.
    d) I often feel defensive or discouraged.

16. When making a health-related decision, what is your approach?
    a) I thoroughly research and consult medical professionals.
    b) I trust my body and instincts.
    c) I talk to friends or family members who have similar experiences.
    d) I make a quick decision based on the most immediate need.

17. How do you decide on a new hobby or activity?
a) I research extensively and evaluate all options.
b) I follow my passion and what excites me.
c) I ask friends or family for suggestions.
d) I try different things spontaneously to see what sticks.

18. How do you deal with uncertainty in decision-making?
a) I gather as much information as possible to reduce uncertainty.
b) I accept uncertainty as a part of life and move forward.
c) I seek reassurance from others.
d) I struggle with uncertainty and may delay making a decision.

19. When working on a group project, what role do you prefer?
a) I like to take the lead and organize the efforts.
b) I contribute my ideas and follow my instincts.
c) I prefer collaborative roles and consensus-building.
d) I am comfortable letting others take the lead.

20. How do you handle long-term goals and planning?
a) I create detailed plans and set specific milestones.
b) I keep a flexible approach and adapt as I go.
c) I discuss my goals with others to get different perspectives.
d) I find it challenging to stick to long-term plans and often change them.

Scoring:
Assign points to each option as follows:
a = 3 points
b = 2 points
c = 1 point
d = 0 points

Evaluate your total score and see which category your decision-making style fits into.

Personality Categories:
Analytical Decision Maker (45-60 points):

You tend to rely on detailed analysis and logical reasoning. You are thorough and methodical, often preferring to have all the information before making a decision.

Intuitive Decision Maker (30-44 points):

You rely on your instincts and gut feelings. You make decisions quickly based on intuition and are comfortable with less information.

Collaborative Decision Maker (15-29 points):

You prefer to involve others in your decision-making process. You value input from different perspectives and often seek consensus.

Spontaneous Decision Maker (0-14 points):

You tend to make quick decisions without overthinking. You may struggle with indecision under pressure and prefer to avoid lengthy deliberation.

CHAPTER SEVENTEEN

Decision- Making Personality Assessment: Scoring & Interpretation

Scoring:

Assign points to each option as follows:

a = 3 points
b = 2 points
c = 1 point
d = 0 points

Evaluate your total score and see which category your decision-making style fits into.

Personality Categories:

Analytical Decision Maker (45-60 points):

You tend to rely on detailed analysis and logical reasoning. You are thorough and methodical, often preferring to have all the information before making a decision.

Intuitive Decision Maker (30-44 points):

You rely on your instincts and gut feelings. You make decisions quickly based on intuition and are comfortable with less information.

Collaborative Decision Maker (15-29 points):

You prefer to involve others in your decision-making process. You value input from different perspectives and often seek consensus.

Spontaneous Decision Maker (0-14 points):

You tend to make quick decisions without overthinking. You may struggle with indecision under pressure and prefer to avoid lengthy deliberation.